# PYTHON PROGRAMMING

## A Smarter and Faster Way To Learn Python In 7 Days

### (With Practical exercises, interview questions, Tips and tricks)

BY

# CHRIS HARVARD

# CONTENTS

Day 1: Moments Before Diving Into The Sea Of Python.................5

What's Python?.................................................................6

Why Python?...................................................................6

What Can Python Do?.........................................................7

How Is Python Different? ....................................................7

Installing The Interpreter ...................................................7

What Is A Program?...........................................................9

A Comparison Of Natural Languages And Programming Languages:
.................................................................................10

What Is Debugging?...........................................................10

Writing Our First *Hello World!* Program: ...............................11

Executing The "Hello World!" Program In Python Interpreter.......12

Ways To Print Values In Python With Print Function .................13

Exercise .......................................................................14

Solution........................................................................15

Day 2: Inside The Big Python Sea .........................................16

Variables.......................................................................17

Variable Naming Conventions................................................17

Types Of Data.................................................................18

Mini Project – A Combined Example Of All Data Types...............23

Dos And Don'ts...............................................................23

Exercises ...................................................................24

Solutions .................................................................24

Operators And Operands .........................................25

The Assignment Operator (=): ..............................25

Comparison Operators ............................................26

Arithmetic Operators ..............................................30

Logical Operators ...................................................31

Membership Operators ...........................................32

Modular Operator ...................................................33

Operator Precedence ...............................................33

Expressions .............................................................34

Compound Assignment Operators .........................34

Comments ..............................................................36

Exercises ................................................................36

Solutions ................................................................36

Day 3: Conditional And Iterative Programming .....38

Code Indentation ...................................................39

Conditional Statements .........................................40

How It Works .........................................................40

Usage And Working Of If, Elif And Else Statements .....41

Code Example .........................................................45

Exercises ................................................................46

Solutions ................................................................47

Loops .......................................................................................... 47

Range (Number) Function ...................................................... 48

Understanding Loop ................................................................ 49

Why Loops Are Important? ...................................................... 52

While Loop ................................................................................ 53

For Loop .................................................................................... 54

Role Of *Continue* And *Break* Statements In Loops ..................... 55

Exercises .................................................................................... 56

Solutions ................................................................................... 59

Mini Project .............................................................................. 59

Day 4: Functions ...................................................................... 61

Functions .................................................................................. 62

Why Functions? ........................................................................ 63

Built-In Functions .................................................................... 64

Basic Syntax .............................................................................. 65

Parameters Or Arguments ........................................................ 65

List And Use Of Common Built-In Functions ......................... 66

Examples ................................................................................... 68

Make Your Own Functions ...................................................... 70

Basic Syntax .............................................................................. 70

How To Define A Function? ..................................................... 71

Use Of Def Keyword ................................................................. 72

How To Call A Function? .......................................................... 72

Code Demonstration ......................................................73

What Are The Advantages Of Functions And Why Functions Are Necessary? ..............................................................74

Switch Case ...............................................................77

The Use Of Get Function ............................................78

Code Example ...........................................................78

If V/S Switch Case Statement – Which Is Better? ...........79

Return Type Functions ...............................................79

Non-Return Type Functions .......................................80

Global Variables .......................................................80

Creating Default Parameter(S) In Functions .................82

Python Lambda Function: ..........................................82

Basic Syntax: ............................................................84

Lambda Arguments: Expression ..................................84

Exercises .................................................................84

Solutions ................................................................85

Day 5: Playing With Strings – String Functions ............86

Importance Of Strings ...............................................87

String Literals: .........................................................88

Assigning A String To A Variable ................................88

Traversing The String Using Loops .............................89

Searching For An Element .........................................91

Indexing And Slicing ................................................91

Negative Indexing ............................................................... 93

Check String: ................................................................... 93

String Concatenation ......................................................... 94

String Functions ............................................................... 95

1. Boolean Methods ........................................................... 95

2. The Use Of Len Keyword ................................................. 98

3. Changing Case Of A String .............................................. 98

4. Replacing A Letter Or Word In A String ............................. 99

5. Splitting A String ........................................................ 100

Exercises ...................................................................... 101

Solutions ..................................................................... 102

Mini Project .................................................................. 102

Day 6: File Handling ........................................................ 104

What Is A File ................................................................ 105

File Handling ................................................................. 105

Opening A File ............................................................... 105

Basic Syntax .................................................................. 106

File Modes In Python ....................................................... 106

Naming: ....................................................................... 107

Creating A File ............................................................... 107

Reading A File ................................................................ 108

Reading The Complete File ................................................ 108

Reading Only Parts Of File ................................................ 109

Reading Lines Of A File..................................................................109

Writing In A File..........................................................................110

Write To An Existing File..............................................................110

Write Lines To An Existing File....................................................111

Closing A File ..............................................................................111

Splitting Lines In A File...............................................................112

Python File Methods ...................................................................112

Exercises .....................................................................................113

Solution ......................................................................................114

Mini Project................................................................................114

Day 7: Data Structures & Object-Oriented Programming............115

Data Structures: ..........................................................................116

List .............................................................................................117

Tuple...........................................................................................121

Creating A Tuple With Only One Item .......................................124

Set ..............................................................................................124

Dictionary...................................................................................127

Nested Dictionaries ....................................................................130

Object-Oriented Programming In Python: ..................................130

Object:.........................................................................................131

Class: ..........................................................................................132

Attributes: ...................................................................................133

Methods: .....................................................................................133

Constructors: ..................................................................... 135

Access Modifiers: ............................................................... 136

Public Access Modifier ...................................................... 137

Private Access Modifier ...................................................... 137

Protected Access Modifier ................................................ 137

Inheritance ......................................................................... 138

Polymorphism .................................................................... 140

Method Overloading........................................................... 141

Method Overriding: ............................................................ 141

Encapsulation ..................................................................... 142

Exercise: .............................................................................. 144

Solution:.............................................................................. 145

Mini Project: ...................................................................... 146

Getting Into The Real World ........................................... 149

Python Tips And Tricks: .................................................... 149

Swapping Two Numbers.................................................... 149

Reversing A String ............................................................. 149

Creating A Single String.................................................... 149

Chaining Of Comparison Operators................................. 150

Print The Path Of The Imported Module ......................... 150

Return Multiple Values From Functions........................... 150

Find The Most Frequent Value In A List ......................... 150

Printing A String N Times ................................................ 151

Transposing A Matrix...................................................151

Combining Two Lists...............................................151

Common Python Questions And Answers:.....................152

Python Project Ideas:................................................155

Dice Rolling Simulator.............................................155

Guess The Number ..................................................155

Url Shortener ..........................................................156

Create A Quiz Application ........................................156

Create A Calculator .................................................157

Bibliography:...........................................................158

# Real Love from Real Students

*"Well, this can definitely be the first time I actually enjoyed a programming book. I am a total non-tech and have absolutely no know-how of coding and programming. Just some Basic knowledge about computers and how to move the mouse lol."* –US Amazon Customer

*"Here are some pros of the book you are about to buy:*

*It is organized in a logical and contained manner. The exercises are effective and fun to do. The examples will help you learn a lot. There are no complex concepts. Everything is simple and easy. It's written in a conversational style. No stupid errors and mistakes to be found. Totally worth the cost."* –US Amazon Customer

*"I am truly impressed by the exercises as to how concise and to the point they are, and how efficiently they help the learner. I personally believe that if I can learn Python like a pro through this book, anybody can. It's just so easy. Or rather, this book makes it so easy."* –US Amazon Customer

*"This book helped me consider how to structure my code. This book hits the nail on its head with on spot perfect teaching methods and examples. By the end of the book, you will be able to use Python Programming to a great extent of not a 100% perfectly. A great book. I even applied to my first machine learning job using python, and I can't wait to read more books from this author."* –US Amazon Customer

# What's in the book?

Before you start reading this book, let us tell you what you will find in it!

This book is carefully (and deliberately) designed for all those who want to master Python Programming using a proven method.

Being way different from all the conventional books, this book not only provides theoretical concepts but also explains real-life examples to help the readers understand Python like a pro. This is extremely important for any successful programmer. Moreover, with the real world coding examples after each theoretical explanation, the book also has exercises along with their solutions for instant feedback within no time.

The whole objective of the book is to not only impart knowledge (quite common with many other books) but also indulge the reader in practical applications. Slowly but surely, it will change your mind to think like a programmer.

And for further assurance, we have added a special section at the end of the book. This additional part is ideal for those who want to get into the real world as soon as possible.

The book also provides real-life interview questions, tips, and tricks (that will help the readers jump-start their careers). Also, the answers and explanations are provided in context with the book.

# What this book ACTUALLY offers?

This book offers:

- ❖ Expert tips on how to code.
- ❖ Python installation guide with visual representations.
- ❖ Interactive coding examples to support your understanding.
- ❖ Exercises at the end of each chapter.
- ❖ Questions, and their answers with reference to the book.
- ❖ Some simple project ideas with the basic instructions to help you get started right after this book.

# So, what's the difference?

You might be thinking what difference does this book make? What makes it stand out in the crowd?

The answer is quite simple. This book is interactive. I know that most of the readers are starting from a very basic level with little or no knowledge on the subject and that they need to learn from the basics.

To resolve these problems, this book holds the hand of the reader and leads them to his journey of Python Programming. The concepts are delivered to the reader in a way as simple as ABC.

We understand that not everyone is a pro at coding and they need to understand the basic concepts in whatever language they're learning. But the main aspect of this book is that it not only takes care of the beginners but also of the coders at the intermediate level.

Just follow the book and practice what is given here. You will soon realize how fast your programming skills develop!

# A few important tips

Here are a few tips before you dive into the whimsical world of programming;

* Here are a few tips before you dive into the whimsical world of programming:
* The best way to learn programming is by doing it.
* Grasp the fundamentals for long term benefits.
* Don't just copy the code, write the code with your own hands.
* Don't be shy to get help. No one's a pro at start.
* In order to get advanced knowledge, don't just stick to one resource. But do not experiment with your time and money. Go after only the reliable resources

# DAY 1

## MOMENTS BEFORE DIVING INTO THE SEA OF PYTHON

# What's Python?

You are not here to know about the Python snake but a programming language called Python. **Python is quite similar to C#, C++, and Java as they are all high-level programming languages. They also use an interactive and object-oriented approach.** What makes Python different is the simplicity of its code which makes it easier for programmers to read, understand and write Python code. The role of a high-level language is to provide an ease to the developer to solve any problem easily in the least number of lines of code, which is then translated in a low-level language (also called machine language). Machine language is understood by machines, and not by humans.

# Why Python?

Though the answers to this question are many, hence, we will cover the major concepts only. The diversified behavior of Python language makes it work in major domain areas such as Gaming, Data Science, Web Development, Software Development, and whatnot. Another major advantage of Python programming language is the "easy-to-integrate" approach so that it goes hand in hand with other programming languages resulting in creating highly-scaled and productive applications.

# What can python do?

Python can be used for creating web applications on a server. In addition to software, Python can be used to build workflows. Python can link to database systems in the database. It can read, write, and edit files as well. It is possible to use Python to manage big data and execute complicated mathematics. Python can be used for quick prototyping or for software development that is ready for production.

# How is Python different?

**Python is intended to be clear and closer to the English language.**

**For example, starting a new line is the way to terminate a program line, instead of semicolons, parentheses etc.** *Another difference is in characterizing a range, Python makes space indentation to define a method. Other programming languages use more complicated syntax like use of braces '{}'.*

# Installing the Interpreter

The role of the interpreter in programming is to run the Python code in a machine. An interpreter is supposed to perform multiple functions such as parsing the source code, translating the code in the machine code format and then executing that interpreted code in the system.

To install Python interpreter, you have to:

> Go to the Python's official website.

   (www.python.org)

> Navigate to Download.

> Here, click the "Download Python [latest version number of Python]" button and you will end up downloading its setup.

- ➢ After downloading it, open File Explorer and navigate to the folder where the setup file is saved after download.
- ➢ Now, open the setup file saved in .exe format and allow it to install all the files in the specified folder.
- ➢ After installation, go to the folder where the files were installed. Here, you will see an executable (.exe) file named "python" with a similar Python logo.
- ➢ Double click on the "python.exe" file, the python interpreter would start to work in your system.

The interpreter will help you run python code or programs.

# What is a program?

**Think of a program as a plan to go for an outing – the first thing you would do will be finding a suitable outing place or spot, then you would arrange the conveyance to travel, and then you would arrive there and have a nice day out. Similarly, a computer program is a step-by-step instruction guide to the computer system about next action.** The program would make a computer work on any computation like solving basic arithmetic expressions, finding an unknown value by solving mathematical equations, searching for an element inside a given set, etc.

# A comparison of natural languages and programming languages:

**Natural languages** are spoken and understood by human. English, French, Arabic, and Dutch are examples of natural languages. In Natural languages, every word possesses a meaning. In natural languages, there are different levels of understanding and contextual meanings for various words.

**Programming languages** are designed to instruct computer about various actions. Programming languages are based on a defined set of rules describing specific concepts. It consists of syntax instead of words. A command line will be understood by computer if its syntax has a clear and precise meaning. Python is also a programming language with defined syntax. If a command line is meant to instruct a computer to do any action then it should be written with proper syntax.

# What is debugging?

In programming languages, a "bug" is an error in the syntax of a computer program that prevents the interpreter to run the code. Debugging is the concept of rectifying bugs in the syntax of a computer program so that the desired action is performed. Debuggers are a type of computer programs which is used to debug a computer program. These debugging programs are also written in programming languages and are used to rectify any bug in the syntax of a program.

# Writing our first *"Hello World!"* program:

If you are new to programming and Python is your first programming language, then you might be thinking why do you have to write a *"Hello, World!"* program. It is a traditional way used to introduce newbies to programming languages. This program simply prints a *"Hello, World!"* message on the display of computer. To do this, open any text editor in your operating system, write *"Hello, World!"* program in your editor. Then save it as first_program.py in your desired folder.

Here is the code of your first Python program:

```
1    print("Hello, World!")
```

Shocked to see just one line? This is the beauty of using Python! Now let's understand what you have written: the **print** is a function that takes data of some type (you will shortly know about datatypes) as a parameter and outputs it on the display.

# Executing the "Hello World!" Program in Python interpreter

To execute the *"Hello World!"* program in the first_program.py file, open command-line (also called "cmd") interface if you are a Windows user or open terminal if you are a Linux user.

To open cmd, press Windows+R to **open** "Run" box. Type **"cmd"** and then click "OK" to **open** a regular **Command** Prompt. Type **"cmd"** and then press Ctrl+Shift+Enter to **open** an administrator **Command** Prompt

Then you have to navigate to the folder where your Python file is saved (the Linux users have to type "chmod a+x first_program.py" in terminal to make the Python file executable). Then write given expression in your command line interface:

$       python ./first_program.py

For Windows use this command:

$       python first_program.py

Congratulations for writing and executing your first program! You would see "Hello, World!" message written on your command-line or terminal interface.

The above command instructs the computer to run the Python interpreter which is already installed and pass the entire file to the interpreter. In return, the interpreter executes the code written in the Python file and returns the output which is shown in the command-line or terminal interface.

# Ways to print values in Python with print function

As we already know, the **print** function is used to print given data on the screen, there is a lot more we can do with this function. Previously, we passed *"Hello, World!"* to the print function which is a combination of alphabets and symbols, we can pass integers and decimal numbers too. The code for this is given below.

For integers:

```
1    print(2)
2    print(666)
```

For decimal numbers:

```
1    print(9.8)
2    print(3.142)
```

Now you might think if we want to print more than one value, do we have to use print function more than once? The answer is no! You can print an infinite number of values using a single print function by separating the value with the help of comma (,) separator. For example:

```
1    print("This is my bag", "Isn't it?")
```

**Output:**

```
This is my bag Isn't it?
```

In addition to simple values, you can also pass an arithmetic expression to this print function and it will display the answer of this expression as output on the screen:

```
1    print(22/7)
```

**Output:**

```
3.142857142857143
```

```
1    print(3*7 + 4*2)
```

**Output:**

```
29
```

It should be noted that while dealing with different arithmetic operators at the same time, Python follows the "BODMAS" rule for operator precedence to solve complex arithmetic expressions involving various arithmetic operators and separators (have a look at this link to understand the "BODMAS" rule: https://en.wikipedia.org/wiki/Order_of_operations).

# Exercise

1) Print your name and a small introduction of yourself.

# Solution

```
1  print("My name is John Doe. I am here to learn Python Programming.")
```

# D A Y   2

## INSIDE THE BIG PYTHON SEA

# Variables

In programming languages, variables are used as temporary data storage areas which help in saving values throughout the entire program execution. Just like the famous "x" in algebra, a variable can have different values throughout a program. As containers of data, **variables help programmers in making programming code flexible and save time.**

# Variable naming conventions

The name of the variable could be anything that should be appropriate and easy to remember. It is better to use a descriptive name to make code understandable. However, it should not start with numbers (from 0 to 9), and any of these symbols (+, -, @, comma, dot, [,], (,)).

Following are the examples of wrong variable names which the Python interpreter will not execute and give an error message:

```
1    1var = "Hello"
```

```
1    v@r = "World"
```

Below is a code example of initializing a variable named "my_var" having the value (also called as data) "Some data"

```
1    my_var= "Some data"
```

The sign (=) is referring that the value "Some data" is assigned to the variable "my_var". Now if you want to use this data further in code, you just have to use the variable name **my_var**.

# Types of data

A program consists of multiple types of data like numbers, strings, lists, objects, etc. This helps the interpreter to know the behavior and working of each data type. In Python, the different data types are:

### *Numeric values*

The numeric values contain any number ranging from $-\infty$ to $+\infty$. Whereas '$\infty$' denotes an infinite value. Numeric values are used in the calculation, but these values are further classified in many categories such as Integers, Long, Float, and Complex.

### *Integers*

An 'Integer' is any number without decimal value. It can be either negative or positive in value. Below is the code of initializing a variable and assigning an integer to it.

```
1    myIntegerVariable = 883
```

## Float

Float is another numeric value that represents real numbers and is written with decimal places. Here is a code example of assigning a float value to a variable:

```
1    myFloatVariable = 883.111
```

## Complex

A complex number is any number that consists of two parts —real and imaginary numbers. The value of an imaginary number is equal to the square root of -1. Usually, a complex number is in the form (A + Bi). Below is the code example of complex numbers:

```
1    myComplexNumberVariable = (5 + 3.121j)
```

You just have to put a "j" or "J" with any float number to make it a complex number.

## String

A string may include a combination of letters, symbols, and/or numbers. Usually, if we want to assign a variable of string type, we must enclose the value in quotes ("value"). **The string is one of the most important data types in programming because many built-in functions use string data structure.**

Here is a code example which assigns a string value to variable name:

```
1      myStringVariable = "82@ab123_-+|{}"
```

You can also store numbers or symbols in form of a string:

```
1      myStringVariable = "12345890"
```

It will not be considered as a numeric value by interpreter, instead, it would be regarded as a string value. Both code lines given below are not considered equivalent to each other by interpreter:

```
1      myStringVariable = "12345890"
```

```
1      myNumberVariable = 12345890
```

**This is because when you write something in quotes, the Python compiler considers it as a chunk of data rather than considering a numeric value because of the quotes. If you are using quotes to describe the value of a variable, the interpreter would understand it as a string.**

## *List*

The list is another important data type in Python where you store data in the form of groups. The concept of lists lies in almost every programming language, but Python is one step ahead of other programming languages. Unlike C#, Java, and C++, Python accepts different natures of data such as integers, floating numbers, and strings in a single list. To implement it, you have to group your data and separate it using comma (,) and finally enclose them in square brackets ([]).

Given below is an example of what we just discussed:

```
1    my_list = ["Beginner to expert", 0, 1, "and", 3.142]
```

Remember that each item in a list lies in its respective address (also called an index). Just like other programming languages, the indexing starts from 0 to n (the total number of items inside a list - 1). To access a particular value, you must know its index.

For example, if you want to access the item "and" in the "my_list" variable, you should know that it is the fourth item in the list which means it has an index of 3 ($4^{th}$ position – 1). This is because the first element has an index of 0. Let's have a quick example of this:

```
1    my_list = ["Beginner to expert", 0, 1, "and", 3.142]
2    print(my_list[3])
```

**Output:**

```
and
```

## *Dictionary*

The dictionary is a data type which shows a slightly different behavior as compared to other data types in Python. In a dictionary, you assign a value to a key so that the next time you want to access a particular value, you must have the key to access it. This makes the data stored securely. To implement a dictionary, you make the key-value pair(s) with the help of the colon (:) and separate them using comma (,). Finally, you encapsulate the whole thing with curly brackets ({}). Let's have a quick demonstration of a dictionary:

*$        my_dictionary = {key1: value1, key2: value2, ...}*

As discussed before, you must know the key to access its value. Remember that both key and value can have different data types. Below is an example of creating a dictionary and accessing one of its values:

```
1    my_dictionary = {1: "One", 2: "Python", "CurrentPythonVersion": 3}
2    print(my_dictionary["CurrentPythonVersion"])
```

**Output:**

3

## Tuples

Tuples are quite similar to lists, but once you set their values, you can't change them like lists. Tuples are used when you want to store constant values and want to use these values as read only (and unchanged) data throughout the whole program. The initialization of tuples is also pretty much the same as lists. The only thing you have to change are brackets; in tuples, you encapsulate the sequence of data in round brackets '()'.

A code example of initialization tuples is:

```
1    my_tuples = ("The sun sets in the east", 9.8, 3.142, "E = MC2")
```

The concept of the list, dictionary, and tuple will be further elaborated in the upcoming chapters.

# Mini Project – a combined example of all data types

Consider a scenario where you want a program that calculates the weight of an object that has a mass of 7.26 kg.

**Solution:**

We know that weight is mass multiplied by gravity (W = mg)

Let's program it!

First, we initialize variables by keeping in mind what value will remain constant throughout a program and what will not:

```
1   constant_values = (9.8)      #Since gravity is constant for every mass
2   mass = 7.26
3   weight = constant_values[0] * mass
4   unit_of_weight = "Newtons"
5   print(weight, unit_of_weight)
```

# Dos and don'ts

1) The name of variables must be related to the value assigned to it and easy to remember.
2) If you have a scenario where multiple values are mapped on to multiple keys, use Dictionary.

3) If you have a combination of related data and you may want to change them, it is always better to use Lists.

4) Do not use tuples if you think you may want to change the values inside the tuples later on.

5) Do not use Lists if you want the data to remain constant throughout the program.

6) Do not use strings if you want to store numbers and use them for calculation purpose.

# Exercises

1) Write a program that calculates and prints the square of the sum of two values (a+b)2. Consider a = 2, and b = 3.

2) Write a program that calculates the value of 'y' in an equation y = 4ax, consider a = 4 and x = 6.

3) Write a program that greets Adam, John, Mosh, and Elisa.

# Solutions

Solution of exercise 1:

```
1    a = 2
2    b = 3
3    square_of_sum = (a+b)*(a+b)
4    print(square_of_sum)
```

Solution of exercise 2:

```
1    a = 4
2    x = 6
3    y_value = 4 * a * x
4    print(y_value)
```

Solution of exercise 3:

```
1    list_of_names = ["Adam", "John", "Mosh", "Elisa"]
2    message = "Welcome"
3    print(message, list_of_names[0])
4    print(message, list_of_names[1])
5    print(message, list_of_names[2])
6    print(message, list_of_names[3])
```

# Operators and operands

**Operators** are symbols that are simply used for calculation between two values and return the final result. Simple example of operators is basic arithmetic operators (+, -, *, and /).

**Operands** are those values that are used in calculations along with the operators.

# The assignment operator (=):

An assignment operator is an equal (=) symbol which is used to assign a value to a variable. For example:

```
1    my_var = "Hello, World!"
```

# Comparison operators

Comparison operators play a major role in the programming field. They are used to compare a value in multiple ways. They tell us whether a certain condition is met or not by returning true or false. If the condition is met, the result is true, if not then you get false.

For comparison operators, let's say if we want to check whether an integer variable has a value between two numbers, we use comparison operators. **Just keep in mind that while using comparison operators, you can only compare two values at a time.**

**For example,**

**'apple' == 'apple'**

Will be true, because both values are similar and equivalent to each other.

As a common programing precedent, the dynamic value (stored as a variable) is placed on the left-hand side of the comparison operator and the static value to be compared is placed on right side of the operator. But if both of the values reside in variables then any of them can be placed on either side of comparison operator. Also, keep in mind that these values must belong to the same data type (it's a good practice but not necessary). Sit tight because there are lots of examples we are going to cover in the later topics. There is a great importance of comparison operators in Python and other programming languages and we will elaborate all of them in detail.

## Equals operator:

An Equal operator is written as **double-equals (==)** sign. It is a comparison operator through which you compare a value (of any type) to any other value. Let's have a quick example to understand the role of Equals operator:

```
1    my_var = "I am some value in string"
2    print(my_var == "I am some value in string")
```

**Output:**

```
True
```

As the left hand and right-hand side are the same.

## Greater than operator:

A **greater than (>)** operator is used when you want to check if the value is greater than some other value. If the condition is met, you get true, otherwise, you get false. It is written as ">" sign. Here is a quick example:

```
1    my_var = 3.142
2    print(my_var > 3)
```

**Output:**

```
True
```

## Greater than and equals operator:

**It is a combination of both greater than and equals comparison operators.** It returns true when the values are either equal or the left side value is greater than the other. It is written as ">=".

Let's jump to the code:

```
1    my_var = 9.8
2    print(my_var >= 9)
```

**Output:**

```
True
```

```
1    my_var = 9.8
2    print(my_var >= 10)
```

**Output:**

```
False
```

## Less than operator:

The opposite of "greater than" operator - it checks whether the value on left side is less than the other. It is written with "<" sign.

Let's look at a short example:

```
1    numeric_val = 999
2    print(numeric_val < 999)
```

**Output:**

```
False
```

## *Less than or equals operator:*

An opposite of "greater than or equals" operator - it returns true by checking whether the value written on left side is less than or equal to the other. It is written as "<=" sign.

A relevant example could be:

```
1    numeric_val = 666
2    print(numeric_val <= 666)
```

**Output:**

```
True
```

## *Not equal operator:*

The **not equal** comparison operator is the complete opposite of the "equal" comparison operator. Here, the conditions are met when one value is not equal to the other. It is written as "!=" sign whereas "!" refers to "not".

Considering a suitable example:

```
1    str = "My name is Josh"
2    print(str != "My name is josh")
```

**Output:**

```
True
```

We can see that the strings in line 1 and 2 are almost equal but shown as not equal to each other. The reason is difference of letter case in both string values. Since "Josh" in the "*str*" variable has a capital "J" on it and "josh" in the string "My name is josh" has a small "j" on it which makes both values non-equivalent and made the "not equal" comparison true. Hence, when comparing strings, the case of letters in string values should be carefully considered.

# Arithmetic operators

Arithmetic operators are standard operators that are used to perform basic calculations between two values. These operators are addition, subtraction, multiplication, and division.

A code example that contains all basic arithmetic operators is:

```
1   value1 = 4
2   value2 = 6
3   addition = value1 + value2
4   subtraction = value1 - value2
5   division = value1 / value2
6   multiplication = value1 * value2
7   print(addition)
8   print(subtraction)
9   print(division)
10  print(multiplication)
```

**Output:**

```
10
-2
0.6666666666666666
24
```

# Logical operators

Logical operators are used in conditional statements. If you want to run a block of code based on inspecting two or more variables, you use logical operators "AND", "OR" or "NOT". They can either return true or false. If the return type is true, the block of code will run. If the return type is false, the block of code will not run.

The names and functions of logical operators are given below:

**AND** – returns true when all of THE assumptions on two or more variables are true. It returns false when any of the assumptions are false.

**OR** – returns true when any one of the assumptions on two or more variables is true. It returns false when all of the assumptions are false.

**NOT** – returns true when the assumption on a variable is false. It returns false when the assumption on a variable is true.

A brief code example:

```
1    print(4 == 4 and 5 == 5)
2    print(4 == 4 or 6 == 5)
3    print(not(1 == 4 and 5 == 5))
```

**Output:**

```
True
True
True
```

Line 1 returns true as both the conditions are true.

Line 2 returns true as one of the conditions is true.

Line 3 returns true as because brackets return false and "not" makes it true.

# Membership operators

It comes from the word "member" as it tests whether a value is a member of a group of members (such as Lists, and Tuples) and generates true or false based on the result. In Python, the membership operators are the keywords "in" and "not in".

Below is a code example for better understanding:

```
1   testing_member = "Josh"
2   list_of_members = ["Adam", "John", "Marie"]
3   print(testing_member in list_of_members)
```

**Output:**

```
False
```

The print statement returns false because Josh is not a member.

# Modular operator

In Python, a modular operator is supposed to return the value of remainder after division of the two operands. Consider an expression "4 % 3", where the remainder is 1 because 4 - 3 * 1 = 1.

```
1    print(4 % 3)
```

**Output:**

```
1
```

# Operator precedence

Precedence of an operator indicates which operator is to be performed first. If all the operators are at the same level, then multiplication and division have higher precedence than addition and subtraction. If there is an expression that contains brackets as well than the operators inside brackets have the highest precedence. Let's summarize this in an example:

```
1    print(5 * 4 - 2 / 4)
```

**Output:**

```
19.5
```

Here, "5 * 4" and "-2 / 4" are solved first because all are at the same level. Now consider an example of the same expression containing brackets:

```
1    print( 5 * (4 - 2) / 4 )
```

**Output:**

```
2.5
```

Here the expression "4 – 2" is solved first because it is in brackets, meaning that it has higher precedence.

# Expressions

Expressions are combinations of operators and operands that are evaluated to become a single value as a result

For example:

$$3 * 4 - 2 / 2 = 11$$

$$9 + 1 - 3 * 2 = 4$$

# Compound assignment operators

**Compound assignment operators are one step ahead of the assignment operator.** In addition to assigning a value to a variable they also perform the calculation with the same variable. They are "+=", "-=", "*=", and "/=".

Let's understand all of them with code examples:

<u>For +=</u>

```
1   val = 5
2   val += 1          # val = val + 1 -> val = 1 + 1 -> val = 2
3   print(val)
```

**Output:**

```
6
```

<u>For −=</u>

```
1   val = 3
2   val -= 2          # val = val - 2 -> val = 3 - 2 -> val = 1
3   print(val)
```

**Output:**

```
1
```

<u>For *=</u>

```
1   val = 2
2   val *= 3          # val = val * 3 -> val = 2 * 3 -> val = 6
3   print(val)
```

**Output:**

```
6
```

<u>For /=</u>

```
1   val = 4
2   val /= 2          # val = val / 2 -> val = 4 / 2 -> val = 2
3   print(val)
```

**Output:**

35

# Comments

**Commenting is the basic concept in Python that is used to provide details to the code. Programmers use commenting to describe the purpose of applying a function in the program.** It is for human understanding purposes thus the Python interpreter ignores them and doesn't recognizes written comments as a part of the program.

To insert comments in a program, write hash symbol (#) as the first character of your statement. For example:

```
1    print(12 * 3)       # twelve is multiplied by three
```

# Exercises

1) Write a program in Python that compares the values of 'a' and 'b' and inverts the result (false becomes true and true becomes false). Whereas, 'a' = 3 and 'b' = 2.

2) Write a program in Python that checks whether "Josh" is on the list and also checks whether "Marie" is not on the list. The list of members is "Josh, Adam, Ervin"

# Solutions

The Solution of exercise 1:

```
1    a = 3
2    b = 2
3    print(not(a == b))
```

## The Solution of exercise 2:

```
1    list = ["Josh", "Adam", "Ervin"]
2    josh = "Josh"
3    marie = "Marie"
4    print(josh in list)
5    print(marie not in list)
6
```

# DAY 3

## CONDITIONAL AND ITERATIVE PROGRAMMING

# Code indentation

Python uses indents. The concept of code indentation plays a major role in Python. Remember, we have not used indenting in any part of code in previous examples. This is because if we do, the Python interpreter will think of it as a part of a code block which is a part of a condition, function, or loop (We will understand each of them shortly).

Your code must follow a consistent indentation such as four whitespaces or tabs. The amount of indentation is your choice, but you must use the same indents throughout that code block. **If you try to indent any line of the code separately, the Python interpreter will throw an error message saying "unexpected indent" and the entire code will not work.** If you want to execute a sequence of code, place the code right before the line starts. The indentation is only done in a block of code that is followed by a condition, function, or loop. Below is an example of writing Python code in a wrong way:

```
1    print("My")
2    print("Name")
3        print("Is")       # "Unexpected indent" error will occur here
4    print("Python")
```

# Conditional statements

In the earlier examples, we have been programming in a **sequential** manner, which means that statements were being performed one after another and followed a sequential pattern. The **conditional statements** modify the sequential approach and are basically used to specify which block of code is to be executed first depending on some condition. **These statements are supposed to return one of the Boolean values (true or false). They identify current value of various variables used in code. These statements are called "conditional" because they work according to the current state of the program.**

# How it works

We have already studied comparison operators and their types in the Day 2 section. Comparison operators are a part of the conditional statement. If a conditional statement returns true then the block of code that is affiliated with it will be executed. If it returns false, then the entire block of code affiliated with it will be ignored by the Python interpreter.

Here is an example for a better understanding of how a conditional statement works. This is just a basic syntax of conditional statements.

```
1  ⊟Condition 1 (expression(s) 1 containing comparison operators)
2        print("hello")
3        print("from")
4        print("the code inside")
5   ⌞    print("condition 1")
6
7  ⊟Condition 2 (expression(s) 2 containing comparison operators)
8        print("hello")
9        print("from")
10       print("the code inside")
11       print("condition 2")
```

**Remember that similar code indentation is used after every condition to denote that it is a part of a similar code block.**

The interpreter will check condition 1 because it comes first before condition 2. If condition 1 is met or simply expression 1 returns true then its block of code will be executed. Thus, the lines print ("hello"), print ("from"), print ("the code inside"), and print ("condition 1") will be executed. Then the interpreter will check condition 2, if the condition does not meet i.e. the expression 2 does not return true, then the lines print("hello") print("from"), print("the code inside"), and print("condition 2") will be completely ignored because they are in the block of condition 2.

# Usage and working of If, elif and else statements

The 'if' statement takes the result of the expression (a condition) and tells the interpreter to execute its block of code if the result of the expression is true. It is written in this way:

41

```
if <condition>:

    Line 1

    Line 2

    ...
```

However, the "if" statement is not bound to take an expression as a condition. You can directly pass Boolean values, numeric values, or strings to it as a condition.

Remember that for Numeric values, the empty values (0, 0.00, ...) will be considered as false, and all the values except empty values (even 0.00000000001) will be considered as true. For strings, the empty string ("") will be considered as false and all the strings except empty strings will have some value in programming languages so they will be considered as true.

The 'elif' statement also works exactly as if statement. The 'elif' statement does not work if there is no if statement placed before it. It consists of "else" and "if". The difference is that the 'elif' statement checks the condition only when the return type of if statement that is placed before it, is false.

Let's have a better understanding of it:

```
if <condition>:
```

line 1 inside *if*

line 2 inside *if*

elif <condition>

line 1 inside *elif*

line 2 inside *elif*

If the condition of '**if**' statement is true, then the interpreter will execute both of the lines inside the '**if' statement** and it will ignore the '**elif' statement** because the first '**if' statement** has been executed.

If the condition of the '**if**' statement is false, then the interpreter will ignore the lines written in the '**if**' block and jump to the '**elif**' statement and see if the condition of the **elif statement** is met. If it is, then the block of '**elif**' **statement** will be executed otherwise ignored (just like **if statement**). You can place as many '**elif**' **statements** (one after another) like:

if <condition>:

// some code

// some code

elif <condition>: (1)

line 1

line 2

elif <condition>: (2)

line 1

line 2

elif <condition>: (3)

line 1

line 2

...

elif <condition>: (n)

line 1

line 2

Each 'elif' statement will only get the interpreter's attention when all of the conditional statements before it, return false. Let's say the first 'elif' gets true, then the interpreter will ignore all upcoming 'elif' statements.

The 'else' is a statement that also contains a block of code to be executed. However, the 'else' statement does not contain any condition. It is placed after 'elif' statement or 'if' statement if there is no 'elif' statement. Its block of code runs only when all the conditions placed before it are identified as false.

In other words, the code block of **else** statement runs when none of the code blocks are executed before **else** statement.

Let's have a better understanding of it:

if <condition>:

        line 1

        line 2

elif <coniditon>:

        line 1

        line 2

else:

        line 1

        line 2

If both the 'if' and 'elif' **statements** are false then regardless of any condition, the code block of the 'else' **statement** will be executed.

# Code example

Enough of the theory! Let's consider a scenario where a variable of numeric type is checked whether it belongs to the range 1 – 10 or 11 – 20. If it belongs to one of the ranges, display the range as output. If it doesn't belong to any range, then show that it is out of range.

```
my_numeric_value = 21
range_1 = "1 - 10"
range_2 = "11 - 20"
if my_numeric_value >= 1 and my_numeric_value<=10:
    print("The range is", range_1)
elif my_numeric_value >= 11 and my_numeric_value<=20:
    print("The range is", range_2)
else:
    print("It is out of range")
```

# Exercises

1) Write a program that calculates the percentage based on total marks and marks obtained and checks:

   a. If the percentage is above or equal to 90, display "A grade".

   b. If the percentage is below 90 but above or equal to 80, display "B grade".

   c. Else, display "F grade".

   Consider total marks = 500 and marks obtained = 450.

2) Write a program that checks if the string has a value:

   a. "Ball", display "Let's play ball".

   b. "Basketball", display "I love Michael Jordan".

c. If it is not equal to any of the strings specified, display "I don't know it".

Consider the string "Volleyball" for comparing.

# Solutions

### Solution of exercise 1:

```
1   total_marks = 500
2   marks_obtained = 450
3   percentage = (marks_obtained / total_marks) * 100
4   if percentage >= 90:
5       print("A grade")
6   elif percentage >= 80 and < 90:
7       print("B grade")
8   else:
9       print("F grade")
```

### Solution for exercise 2:

```
1   string_test = "Volleyball"
2   if string_test == "Ball":
3       print("Let's play ball")
4   elif string_test == "Basketball":
5       print("I love Michael Jordan")
6   else:
7       print("I don't know it")
```

# Loops

Loops are used to execute lines of code $n^{th}$ number of times. Now some of you might think why would one want to execute the same code again and again? This is because there is a bit of logic involved inside the usage of loops (which we will cover shortly). A cycle of executing a block of code is also called an iteration.

# Range (number) function

The **range** function inside loops informs the Python interpreter how many times a number of instructions should be executed.

The **range** function works this way:

$       range (start_number, stop_number, number_of_incremets/decrements)

For example, we want to define a range from 2 to 5 having an increment of 1:

```
1       range(2, 6, 1)
```

The range will be 6 – 2 = 4, which means it starts from 2 and ends to 5 (2, 3, 4, and 5 – ascending order).

If we change the number of increments to 2 in the above example:

```
1       range(2, 6, 2)
```

Then the generated sequence will be 2 and 4. Every next number is equal to the previous number incremented by 2.

**<u>Note:</u>**

The start number and number of increments/decrements are optional. If we don't provide the start number, then the Python interpreter considers it as '0' by default. If we don't provide the number of increments or decrements, then the Python interpreter considers it as '1' by default.

Consider an example in which the sequence is generated in descending order – from a large number to a small number:

```
1       range(6, 2, -1)
```

**The -1 in the 3rd argument shows that the number is going to be decreased. The range here is also 6 – 2 = 4 but the difference is that the start number "6" is greater than the stop number "2" so the generated sequence is in descending order that is by reducing the previous value by 1 to generate the next value. Here, the sequence is 6, 5, 4, and 3.**

# Understanding loop

First of all, lets understand the structure of loops:

$       loopName iterator_variable in range_of_iterator_numbers:

$               line 1 inside loop

$               line 2 inside loop

$               line 3 inside loop

$                    ...

$          # End of loop

As described, loops are used to execute a block of code again and again (till 'n' times). When the Python interpreter sees the name of the loop, it concludes that it is going to execute commands a number of times defined by the **range** function.

<u>The code flow</u>:

In the following example, there are three lines of code inside a loop. The range defined by the **range** function is 3: 0, 1, and 2.

```
1   loopName x in range(3):
2       print(x*2)
3       print(x*3)
4       print(x*4)
5
6   #End of loop
```

When the Python interpreter reads the "loopName", it takes the first number generated from the sequence by range function (that is "0" in this example) and assigns it to the variable "x". Now the current value of "x" is 0 in the loop.

The program lines written in the loop are as below:

```
2       print(x*2)
3       print(x*3)
4       print(x*4)
```

By considering the current value of "x" as 0, we get the output:

| | |
|---|---|
| 0 | # print(0*2) |
| 0 | # print(0*4) |
| 0 | # print(0*6) |

Now after the execution of all lines, the Python interpreter goes back to its initial stage where the loop is defined and takes the second value from the sequence (that is "1") and again assigns it to the variable "x". Now, inside the loop, the "x" holds the value 1. Thus, after executing the lines:

```
2        print(x*2)
3        print(x*3)
4        print(x*4)
```

We get the output, considering the current value of "x" as 1:

| | |
|---|---|
| 2 | # print(1*2) |
| 4 | # print(1*4) |
| 6 | # print(1*6) |

Again, the Python interpreter goes back to its initial stage where the loop is defined and takes the third value from the sequence (that is "2"). Now the value that the variable "x" holds is 2. Thus, by executing these three lines of code again, we see the output:

| | |
|---|---|
| 4 | # print(2*2) |
| 8 | # print(2*4) |

| 12 | # print(2*6) |

Finally, the combined output that we will get on our screen is:

| 0 | # print(0*2) |
| 0 | # print(0*4) |
| 0 | # print(0*6) |
| 2 | # print(1*2) |
| 4 | # print(1*4) |
| 6 | # print(1*6) |
| 4 | # print(2*2) |
| 8 | # print(2*4) |
| 12 | # print(2*6) |

This is how the loop works.

# Why loops are important?

❖ Loops are the core concept of every programming language and same is the case with Python. There are countless benefits of using loops but generally, loops are important because of the following reasons:

- ❖ They make the code super small and understandable, making the Python interpreter work more for the programmer.
- ❖ If you want to execute a block of code a million times, you will have to write millions of commands by yourself. This is why the use of loops would be necessary.
- ❖ Loops are often used while working with lists, objects, and dictionaries. Their work is to dynamically iterate through elements of lists and key-value pairs of dictionaries.
- ❖ They play a vital part in building logic to solve problems efficiently.

# While loop

The **while** loop is a type of loop in which the block of code runs on behalf of a condition. The sequence of code keeps on repeating until the condition generates false. There is no **range** function in **while** loop so you have to specify start value, stop value, and numbers of increment/decrement by yourself.

Let's consider an example in which we display each element of the sequence "0, 1, 2, 3, 4" line by line using while loop:

```
iterator = 0        # Sets the start value to 0.
while iterator < 5: # Declaring while loop with a stop value of 6.
    print(iterator) # Displaying the current value of the variable "iterator".
    iterator = iterator + 1    # Incrementing the value of the variable "iterator" by 1.
```

# For loop

The 'for' loop is a type of loops in which you can specify the start value, stop value, and incrementing/decrementing value using the **range** function.

Let's consider an example in which we display the numbers "0, 2, 4, 6, 8, 10" in just two lines using for loop:

```
1  for iterator in range(0, 11, 2):
2      print(iterator)
```

The 'for' loop is also used to iterate over a list of elements.

Consider an example that prints all the elements of a list using for loop:

```
1  list_of_veggies = ["Broccoli", "Corn", "Cucumber", "Lettuce", "Pumpkin"]
2  for vegetable in list_of_veggies:
3      print(vegetable)
```

You get the output on screen:

```
Broccoli
Corn
Cucumber
Lettuce
Pumpkin
```

Using 'for' loop, you can also iterate over a dictionary of key-value pairs using the function **items ()**.

Consider an example of getting key-value pairs one by one in the dictionary and printing the key and value of each key-value pair individually.

```
1    my_dictionary = {1:"one", 2:"two", 3:"three"}
2    for current_key, current_value in my_dictionary.items():
3        print(current_key, current_value)
```

You get the output on screen:

```
1 one
2 two
3 three
```

# Role of *continue* and *break* statements in loops

The **break** statement is used when you want to come out from a loop in the middle of the code block. Consider a scenario in which you want to iterate through each element in a list of vegetables and start displaying the names of vegetables until you find the vegetable name "Lettuce":

```
1    list_of_veggies = ["Broccoli", "Corn", "Cucumber", "Lettuce","Pumpkin"]
2    for vegetable in list_of_veggies:
3        if vegetable == "Lettuce":
4    # After executing the break statement
5    #the interpreter ignores all instructions after this statement inside loop.
6            break
7        print(vegetable)
```

The **continue** statement is the opposite of the **break** statement. It tells the Python interpreter to keep on executing the loop. Consider a scenario in which you want to iterate through a list of numbers and when you get number "1", you increase the counter by 1 and continue executing the code until you get the number "2":

```python
list_of_numbers = [1,3,5,1,1,4,1,2,1,1,1]
counter_of_one = 0
for x in list_of_numbers:
    if x == 1:
        counter_of_one = counter_of_one + 1
        continue
    if x == 2:
        break
print(counter_of_one)
```

# Exercises

1) Write a program that exchanges the values of two dictionaries that contain the same keys. The dictionaries could be anything but for now, consider:

   dictionary_a = {"A": "Apple", "B": "Ball", "C": "Cat"}

   dictionary_b = {"A": "Ant", "B": "Basket", "C": "Carrot"}

   After executing the program, the dictionaries should become:

   dictionary_a = {"A": "Ant", "B": "Basket", "C": "Carrot"}

   dictionary_b = {"A": "Apple", "B": "Ball", "C": "Cat"}

2) Write a program that takes an integer inside the list of positive integers and prints it in this way:

If there is an integer "5", the program has to print "5" five times.

If there is an integer "2", the program has to print "2" two times.

The elements inside the list of positive integers may vary but for now, consider the list:

list_of_positive_integers = [2,5,6,3,2,1,6]

After the program execution, you get the following output:

2

2                         # The number "2" is displayed two times

5

5

5

5

5                         # The number "5" is displayed five times

```
6

6

6

6

6

6          # The number "6" is displayed six times

3

3

3          # The number "3" is displayed three times

2

2          # The number "2" is displayed two times

1          # The number "1" is displayed one time

6

6

6

6          # The number "6" is displayed six times
```

# Solutions

### Solution of Exercise 1:

```
1    dictionary_a = {"A": "Apple", "B": "Ball","C": "Cat"}
2    dictionary_b = {"A": "Ant", "B": "Basket","C": "Carrot"}
3
4    temp = ""
5
6    for k_a,v_a in dictionary_a.items():
7        temp = dictionary_b[k_a]
8        dictionary_b[k_a] = v_a
9        dictionary_a[k_a] = temp
10
11   for k_a,v_a in dictionary_a.items():
12       print(k_a, v_a)
13
14   for k_b,v_b in dictionary_b.items():
15       print(k_b, v_b)
```

### Solution of Exercise 2:

```
1    list_of_positive_integers = [2,5,6,3,2,1,6]
2
3    for number in list_of_positive_integers:
4        for x in range(number):
5            print(number)
```

# Mini project

You have two integer variables – start number and stop number. These variables can have a random integer value. If the start number is less than stop number, you have to iterate from start number to stop number with an increment of 1. If the start number is greater than stop number, you have to iterate upside down - from stop number to start number with a decrement of 1.

Now, in each iteration, you have to check whether the current number is even or odd. If the number is even, increase the value of the even counter by 1. If odd, increase the value of the odd counter by 1. Finally, check which of them (even and odd counters) is greater. After checking, print the greater counter. Consider the start number be '13' and stop number be '4' for now.

```
1    start_number = 13
2    stop_number = 4
3
4    even_counter = 0
5    odd_counter = 0
6
7    set_increment_or_decrement = 0   # Default value
8
9    def checkEvenOrOdd(num):
10       if num % 2 == 0:
11           return "Even"
12       else:
13           return "Odd"
14
15   if(start_number < stop_number):
16       set_increment_or_decrement = 1   # Increment of 1
17   else:
18       set_increment_or_decrement = -1 # Decrement of 1
19
20   for x in range(start_number, stop_number, set_increment_or_decrement):
21       print(x)
22       if checkEvenOrOdd(x) == "Odd":
23           odd_counter = odd_counter + 1
24       if checkEvenOrOdd(x) == "Even":
25           even_counter = even_counter + 1
26
27   if even_counter > odd_counter:
28       print("Even counter is greater")
29   else:
30       print("Odd counter is greater")
```

# DAY 4

## FUNCTIONS

# Functions

In the earlier sections, we have been programming at the basic level. Functions are one of the most important things to learn in Python and will take us to the next level.

A function is a part of a program that can perform tasks. A function contains multiple lines of code which could be executed whenever there is a need of use. A function has a name so that it is easier for us to call it.

**Functions are categorized in two types; built-in functions and user-defined functions. Functions can receive and send values. The value that we pass in a function is also called an *argument*.** As mentioned, the code inside function is indented.

The pseudo code structure given below gives an idea about how a function looks like:

function      myfunc(*argument*):          #creating a function of name "myfunc"

    Line 1 inside function          #code inside function starts here

    Line 2 inside function

    Line 3 inside function

    ...

```
my_var = "abc"                    #code outside function
```

# Why functions?

Functions are a small piece of programs that are supposed to do their work dynamically. It is independent of the program and can be used whenever and wherever we want.

There are many benefits of using functions. Some of the advantages are listed below:

- Reduces duplication of code.

- Increases code reusability.

- Increases the readability of the code.

- Decomposition of complex code into simpler modules.

- It also saves quite a lot of time.

For example, if we want to add two integer variables ten times, we don't have to write the logic of addition ten times. Instead, we create a function that takes two integers and returns its sum. Now we have to only call this function and pass two integers as arguments and get their sum. Hence, the function makes the code reusable and there will be fewer chances of experiencing human error. Let's understand why functions are used.

Program 1

```
1    var_a = 1
2    var_b = 2
3    print(var_a + var_b)          # You get 3
4    var_a = var_a + 1             # var_a = 2
5    var_b = var_b + 1             # var_b = 3
6    print(var_a + var_b)          # You get 5
```

But a simpler and intelligent approach could be:

## Program 2

```
1    func    addFunction(integer_1, integer_2):
2        return integer_1 + integer_2
3
4    var_a = 1
5    var_b  = 2
6    print(addFunction(var_a, var_b))    # Both variables are passed in function as arguments
7                                        # and their sum is returned and printed
8                                        #with print function, thus you get 3.
9
10   var_a = var_a + 1
11   var_b = var_b + 1
12   print(addFunction(var_a, var_b))    # You get 5
```

# Built-in functions

A built-in function is a function that is already created by Python interpreter. We can't modify it. We can just use it and perform a task. The **print** function is a well-known example of built-in functions. It is not our concern what lines of code are written inside the **print** function; we just use it to perform the task. There are numerous built-in functions in Python.

# Basic syntax

Built-in functions are called according to the requirement of the code. They are called by their name and in parenthesis, we just pass some arguments as input statements. Passing these parameters is entirely optional. The basic syntax to call a built-in function is:

*built_in_function_name (argument1, argument 2, . . .)*

# Parameters or Arguments

*The information that is passed to a function is called a parameter or an argument. There can be multiple arguments within the parenthesis, just after the function's name. You have to separate each argument/parameter with a comma. Consider the following example:*

```
1  def my_function(fname):
2      print(fname + "Doe")
3
4  my_function("John")
5  my_function("Jane")
```

*Output:*

```
JohnDoe
JaneDoe
```

*Here in this example, the function has one parameter, "fname". When the function is called, we pass on the name "John" and "Jane" as the parameters.*

*The function the perform string concatenation method to add "Doe" after the parameters passed.*

We can also set a default parameter; in case any other parameter is not passed to the function. Consider the same example:

```
1  def my_function(fname = "James"):
2      print(fname + "Doe")
3
4  my_function("John")
5  my_function()
6  my_function("Jane")
```

Output:

```
JohnDoe
JamesDoe
JaneDoe
```

Here, we set "James" as the default parameter. Whenever any parameter is not called, "James" will be used as a default parameter of the above function.

# List and use of common built-in functions

Here is the list of some commonly used built-in functions in Python:

| Function | Use |
|---|---|
| abs() | returns the absolute value of a numerical value |
| bin() | returns binary value of a numerical value |

| | |
|---|---|
| **bool()** | returns Boolean value |
| **eval()** | evaluates the code within the program |
| **float()** | returns the floating point number of a value. |
| **hash()** | returns the hash value of an object. |
| **hex()** | returns hexadecimal value of the number. |
| **id()** | returns the id of an object |
| **input()** | reads and returns a line of string |
| **int()** | returns an integer of a value |
| **len()** | returns the length of the specified object |
| **list()** | returns a list |
| **max()** | returns the maximum value |
| **min()** | returns the minimum value |
| **next()** | returns the next item from an iterator. |
| **pow()** | returns x to the power y value |
| **print()** | prints the specified object |
| **range()** | return sequence of integers between starting and stopping value |

| sort() | sorts the given list |
|---|---|
| str() | returns string objects |
| sum() | returns the sum of an iterator |
| type() | returns the type of an object |

# Examples

Enough of the theory! Here are some fun examples to help you understand the functions better.

- **abs()** – Returns the positive value of the number.

```
1    print(abs(-3.142))
```

**Output:**

```
3.142
```

- **len()** – Returns the length of strings, lists, and objects.

```
1    print(len("abcdefghijklmnopqrstuvwxyz"))
```

**Output:**

```
26
```

- **sum()** – Returns the sum of numbers inside the list of numbers.

```
1    list_of_numbers = [1,3,5,7,9]
2    print(sum(list_of_numbers))
```

**Output:**

25

- **min()** – Returns the smallest number inside list of numbers.

```
1    list_of_numbers = [1,3,5,7,9]
2    print(min(list_of_numbers))
```

**Output:**

1

- **max()** – Returns the largest number inside list of numbers.

```
1    list_of_numbers = [1,3,5,7,9]
2    print(max(list_of_numbers))
```

**Output:**

9

- **round(number, decimal_places)** – Returns the rounded number up to 'n' decimal places.

```
1    print(round(1.4444, 2))
```

**Output:**

# Make your own functions

Just like you write a program to perform a task, you can also create your own functions to perform sub-tasks as they are nothing but a sub-program. For example, we are human as programs and functioning like a human being is what we are supposed to do, so this is our main task. Any human task, includes sub-tasks such as speaking, seeing, listening, running, dancing, etc. We can perform these things whenever we want.

Python has many built-in functions like print (), etc. but you can also create your own functions. It is necessary to declare all the functions at the start because as we know the Python interpreter starts reading lines of code from top to bottom so it must have all the information regarding functions (name and commands inside it) in its memory from the very beginning.

**Thus, later when it sees some code that uses the functions, it must know what function is being called. Hence, there is no doubt left for the Python interpreter to execute that command (calling a user-defined function).**

# Basic syntax

The basic syntax of a function is:

*def function_name(argument1, argument2, . . .):*

*"""function_docstring"""*

*statement_1*

*statement_2*

*. . . .*

*return [expression]*

# How to define a function?

Defining the function is very easy as long as you play by the rules. You can define any type of function with any type of input arguments. So, first, let's learn the steps that we need to follow in order to build our functions. Just keep the above syntax in mind.

1   Use the keyword "**def**" at the beginning of defining any function.

2   Follow this up with your function's name.

3   Provide the input parameters in the parenthesis. It is entirely optional and depends on the task required to be performed by the function. There can be multiple parameters/arguments.

4   Put a colon after closing the parenthesis. This marks the end of the function header.

5    "function_docstring" is also an optional string. It is used to describe what our defined function does.

6    The statements make up the body of the function. There can be more than one statement in a function. All the statements are indented at the same level.

7    In the end, there is an optional return statement. It provides the output value from the function.

Just keep the above 7 steps in mind and you are good to go.

# Use of def keyword

The 'def' keyword tells Python interpreter that a user-defined function is going to be initialized (We will shortly understand what user-defined functions are). The 'def' is short of the word "define" and it is written before the name of function so that the Python interpreter considers the name as function's name.

# How to call a function?

Now that you have learned to build a function, then comes the next step i.e. calling a function. Calling a function is even easier than building one. After you have built a function just treat them like the built-in functions that we have discussed before.

The basic syntax to call a function is as follows:

*function_name(arg1, arg2)*

# Code demonstration

Let's just consider a human as a program:

Program Name: Human

```
1   # Defining functions of listening, speaking, walking and running
2   def listen(some_msg):
3       print("Listening:",some_msg)
4       return
5
6   def speak(some_msg):
7       print("Speaking:",some_msg)
8       return
9
10  def walk():
11      print("Wakling")
12      return
13
14  def run():
15      print("Running")
16      return
17
18
19  # Now calling the functions
20  listen("I need to go")
21  speak("He threw three free throws")
22  walk()
23  run()
```

**Output:**

```
Listening: I need to go
Speaking: He threw three free throws
Wakling
Running
```

# What are the advantages of functions and why functions are necessary?

The main advantage of creating functions is that you don't have to write (For example) "print ("Walking")" whenever you need it. You just create a function and inside it, you place this Python command (print ("Walking")), and execute this command by just calling the function's name.

It is necessary because real-world applications contain thousands of commands, which means the more there will be commands, the bigger it will have memory size. This results in making programs less efficient because if there is a lot of code the Python interpreter has to go through, definitely it will generate results not as fast as we expect.

To make a program efficient, you have to reduce the size of the code. For this, you first identify the duplicate commands in your program and combine them to become a single function that is doing the task for all of them with perfection. This reduces the chances of getting human errors as well because once you define the task in your custom function, you can use it a hundred times with a hundred percent perfection.

You can even make your function dynamic so that it can get different values and then generates the output based on different values. Let's consider a code example of calculating velocity in both efficient and inefficient ways. The formula to calculate it is distance (S) divided by time (t).

## Program 1 – An inefficient approach

```
1    distance = 500 (meters)
2    time = 3 (minutes)
3    velocity = distance / time
4    print (velocity)          # You get the value 166.6666 approximately
5
6    # Calculating again with different values
7    distance = 1500 (meters)
8    time = 6 (minutes)
9    velocity = distance / time
10   print (velocity)          # You get the value 250
11
12   # Calculating again with different values
13   distance = 2500 (meters)
14   time = 9 (minutes)
15   velocity = distance / time
16   print (velocity)          # You get the value 277.77 approximately
17
18   # Calculating again with different values
19   distance = 3500 (meters)
20   time = 12 (minutes)
21   velocity = distance / time
22   print (velocity)          # You get the value 291.66 approximately
```

# Total lines of program 1 excluding comments: 16 (four lines of code to calculate velocity * number of velocities to be calculated)

## Program 2 – An efficient approach

```
1   def printVelocity(distance, time):
2       print(distance/time)
3       return
4
5   # Considering the same distance and time as in Program 1
6   distance = 500 (meters)
7   time = 3 (minutes)
8   print(printVelocity(distance, time))
9
10  #Changing values of distance and time
11  distance = 1500 (meters)
12  time = 6 (minutes)
13  print(printVelocity(distance, time))
14
15  # Changing values of distance and time
16  distance = 2500 (meters)
17  time = 9 (minutes)
18  print(printVelocity(distance, time))
19
20  # Changing values of distance and time
21  distance = 3500 (meters)
22  time = 12 (minutes)
23  print(printVelocity(distance, time))
```

Total lines of program 1 excluding comments:

*15 (three lines of code to calculate velocity * number of velocities to be calculated + 3 lines of code to define a function)*

Note that if your program has to create velocity a hundred times then the number of lines you have to write by following the approach as of Program 1:

*4 (number of lines to calculate velocity) * 100 (number of velocities to be calculated)*

*= 400 lines.*

And if you follow the approach of Program 2:

*3 (number of lines to calculate velocity) \* 100 (number of velocities to be calculated) + 3 (number of lines to define a function)*

*= 3 \* 100 + 3*

*= 303 lines*

Consider the differences in the number of lines between the two programs and you will have your answer that which approach is efficient and should be followed

# Switch case

Don't confuse with the keyword "**switch**" used in other programming languages because Python doesn't know the keyword **switch**. But it has the same concept that is comparing a value with multiple values. In Python, a switch case is simply a dictionary inside a function that contains key-value pairs.

Now some of you may question why it is necessary to encapsulate a dictionary in a function. The answer is that in the world of functional programming, it is always a best practice to declare sensitive information inside functions. As we know a dictionary is used to secure the data (values), consider a dictionary that contains very sensitive information that you never want to update or delete any element inside it. All you want is to show the values according to their keys, nothing else.

If you initialize this dictionary outside a function, there will be no restriction of updating and deleting items inside the dictionary as it is initialized globally (you will understand the concept of global and local variables shortly). The solution is to encapsulate it inside a function to secure its integrity and restrict it from taking any built-in functions which may damage its integrity.

# The use of get function

The 'get' function fetches the value from a dictionary based on the given key and if the key isn't found in the dictionary, then it provides an alternate value to the user in order to maintain its user-friendly behavior.

# Code example

Consider a dictionary that contains U.S. citizen's telephone numbers based on their names. Remember that in this example, the programmer just wants to restrict the numbers to only show:

```
1  dic = {"A":1, "B":2}
2  print(dic.get("A"))
3  print(dic.get("C"))
4  print(dic.get("C","Not Found ! "))
```

**Output:**

```
1
None
Not Found !
```

# If v/s Switch Case statement – which is better?

The 'if' statement is used when:

You want to compare a variable to a shortlist of values.

You want to involve any comparison operator (except "==") then the usage of the 'if' **statement** is preferred.

Any kind of restriction inside data is not needed.

The **Switch Case** statement is used when:

You want to compare a variable to a very long list of values.

You just want to use a double-equals comparison operator.

You want the information to be restricted.

# Return type functions

Functions that provide some value so that it can be used later outside functions are called return type functions as they are returning some value after being called. Consider the format of return type functions:

```
def squareOfNumber(number):
    return number * number
    square_of_two = squareOfNumber(2)

print(square_of_two)
```

**Output:**

4

# Non-return type functions

Functions that do not provide any value and perform all the tasks (such as displaying) by itself are called non-return type functions. Consider the format of non-return type functions:

```
1   def displaySquareOfNumber(number):
2       print(number * number)
3
4   displaySquareOfNumber(2)
```

**Output:**

4

# Global variables

Variables that are declared outside functions, loops, or conditional statements are called Global Variables.

$   *def   someFunction():*

$          *...*

$      *this_is_a_global_variable = "Some value"*

$      *this_is_another_global_variable = "Some value"*

However, the global variables can be accessed inside functions, loops, or conditional statements. Consider an example:

```
1    a_global_variable = 2
2    another_global_variable = 4
3    def multiplier():
4        return a_global_variable * another_global_variable
5    print(multiplier())
```

**Output:**

8

Local variables

Variables that are declared inside functions, loops, or conditional statements are called Local Variables.

$        def        someFunction():

$                this_is_a_local_variable = "Some value"

$                this_is_another_local_variable = "Some value"

                # End of function here

$                this_is_a_global_variable = "Some value"

However, the local variables can't be accessed outside functions, loops, or conditional statements. Consider an example:

```
1    def someFunction():
2        a_local_variable = "Some value"
3        another_local_variable = "Some value"
4
5    print (a_local_variable)        # Here you will get an error
```

**Output:**

```
NameError: name 'a_local_variable' is not defined
...
```

# Creating default parameter(s) in functions

There is also a concept of getting a default value in a function as a parameter if the value is not provided when the function is being called. Let's consider an example of getting a default value in an argument named "myName" inside the function:

```
1   def printName(myName = "No name"):
2       print(myName)
3
4   printName()
5   printName("Alexander")
```

**Output:**

```
No name
Alexander
```

# Python Lambda function:

A lambda function in python is an anonymous function that can take any number of arguments but can only have one expression.

An anonymous function is a function without a name. The 'def' keyword is used to define the normal functions and the lambda keyword is used for anonymous functions.

Let's try to understand the difference between a normal 'def' defined function and lambda function by examples.

```
def square(x):
    return x*x

print(square(3))
```

*Output*

```
9
```

Now let's try using the lambda function.

```
f = lambda x: x*x
print(f(3))
```

*Output*

```
9
```

The difference is quite obvious. Both of the programs return the square of a given number. But, when we use def, the function must be defined with any name like 'square' and we also need to pass a parameter to it. After executing the function, the output of the function must be returned to from where the function was called using the return keyword.

Lambda's definition does not have a "return" statement, it only has an expression which is returned. A lambda definition can be put anywhere a function is expected, and its assignment to a variable at all is not required at all. This is the level of simplicity of lambda functions.

# Basic Syntax:

The functions have distinct arguments (number) and they all have one illustration. This helps us in assessing the expression and resetting the function afterward. Wherever work objects are needed, the lambda function is helpful.

Following is the syntax of lambda functions:

# lambda arguments: expression

Using lambda functions is useful when you need to build a nameless function for a smaller span of time. Lambda is used as an argument in Python. Keep in mind that in the event of other functions, the higher-order functions are simply those regarded as arguments.

# Exercises

1) Create a function that takes two parameters: (1) first name and (2) last name and prints the full name by combining the first name and last name. You have to place the string "Hello" before the full name. For example, "Hello Albert Einstein".

2) Create a function that takes an operator symbol (for example: +, -, *, /) as parameter. Inside the function, you have to check the given operator with the list of operators that you have created inside the function and if the given operator is found inside the list, return the operator in English. For example, if we pass "+" as parameter, we get "Addition". If the operator is not found, return the string "Operator not found".

# Solutions

### The Solution to exercise 1:

```
1  def printFullName(first_name, last_name):
2      print("Hello",first_name,last_name)
3
4  printFullName("James", "Bond")
```

### The Solution to exercise 2:

```
1  def symbolToEnglish(operator_symbol):
2      operator_list = {
3      "+" : "Addition",
4      "-" : "Subtraction",
5      "*" : "Multiplication",
6      "/" : "Division",
7      }
8      return operator_list.get(operator_symbol, "Operator not found")
9
10 print(symbolToEnglish("/"))
```

# DAY 5

## PLAYING WITH STRINGS – STRING FUNCTIONS

# Importance of Strings

Strings are the most important data type because they are used in pretty much every scenario. We need strings when we want to show relevant information to the user. For example, warnings, prompts, announcements, conclusions, results that can be read by humans.

**If we just show the results in numbers to the user without referring to where do this numerical data come from, how will the user understand? Hence, if we want to display the count of odd and even integers from a list of numbers:**

If the output is given like this:

3

4

Will a user be able to tell which the count is of even and which is the count of odd integers from the list?

When we add some descriptive text before it, then the user will be able to identify context clearly, like this output is written:

*The count of even integers: 3*

*The count of odd integers: 4*

We create computer programs for the ease of humans. If humans aren't able to understand the output of the computer program, then what's the point of creating a program?

If you want to store someone's name, address, phone number, marital status, job position, hobbies, and almost everything that cannot be specified in numbers, you are required to use strings.

Strings are also used in validation and computation. We will be going through many examples in the upcoming sections.

# String Literals:

Either single quotation marks or double quotation marks surround the string literals in python. 'Hello' is the same as "Hello". You can use the print () function to display a string literal.

# Assigning a string to a variable

We can assign strings to variables just like any other data type.

```
1    a = "Hello"
2    print(a)
```

*Output:*

Hello

*Multiline String*

We can also assign a multi-line string to a single variable by using three quotation marks.

```
1  a = """Lorem ipsum dolor sit amet,
2  consectetur adipiscing elit,
3  sed do eiusmod tempor incididunt
4  ut labore et dolore magna aliqua."""
5  print(a)
```

*Output:*

```
Lorem ipsum dolor sit amet,
consectetur adipiscing elit,
sed do eiusmod tempor incididunt
ut labore et dolore magna aliqua.
```

Strings in Python are arrays of bytes depicting Unicode characters like many other common programming languages.

# Traversing the string using loops

As mentioned above, strings are not only used for displaying information, we can also validate the data stored in memory and make its integrity even better by traversing the data (in strings) with the help of loops. By traversing, we mean getting every single character of the string so that we may use them as a part of our logic to make the quality of data better.

For now, let's just traverse a string "Hello, World!" and print each character of it using a loop:

```
1    my_str = "Hello, World!"
2
3    for char in my_str:
4        print(char)
```

We will get the output like this:

```
H
e
l
l
o
,

W
o
r
l
d
!
```

Here, the Python interpreter converts the string into the list of characters. After that, it starts picking each alphabet from left to right and assigns to the variable "char". Thus, at first, it picks the letter "H" from "Hello, World!" as it is the first letter of the string. Then it picks "e" as a second letter. After picking all the letters of the string "Hello, World!", finally it gets "!" as the last character of the string. When it finds that there is no other character after "!", it jumps out of the loops.

But what we are going to do with these letters? We will get to know about it in further topics.

# Searching for an element

In some situations, we have to know how many times an alphabet is included in a string. Let's create a program that calculates the count of letter 's' inside a string "There is no such thing as a free lunch.":

```
alphabet_count = 0
my_str = "There is no such thing as a free lunch."
my_char = "s"

for alphabet in my_str:
    if alphabet == my_char:
        alphabet_count = alphabet_count + 1

print (alphabet_count)
```

**Output:**

3

# Indexing and Slicing

Indexing in strings is pretty much similar to indexing in the list. Consider a string "Python" that contains 6 letters. We can access each letter by providing the index number after the string variable. A very important thing to remember here is that, just like the lists, the index in strings also starts from "0".

For example, if we want to access the letter "P" inside a string "Python", we know that it is in the first index that is 0. Let's create a program that accesses all the elements of the string "Python" by providing the index number of each letter inside a string:

```
my_str = "Python"
print(my_str[0])        # Gets "P"
print(my_str[1])        # Gets "y"
print(my_str[2])        # Gets "t"
print(my_str[3])        # Gets "h"
print(my_str[4])        # Gets "o"
print(my_str[5])        # Gets "n"
```

**Output:**

P
y
t
h
o
n

We can also provide the range of index numbers to a string to get the letters in the form of a substring. This is called slicing a string as we are getting the chunks of strings as a substring. Let's slice a string "Python" to get substrings like "Pyth", "thon", "ytho", "Py", "on". First, let's create a string 'Python'

```
my_str = "Python"
```

# To get the substring "Pyth", we have to provide a range of four indexes "0, 1, 2, 3" – from 0 to 4 (4 is the point at which the Python interpreter will stop getting more characters so the index 4 is not included in fetching the character from the string).

```
1    print(my_str[0:4]) # You get the substring "Pyth"
2    print(my_str[2:6]) # You get the substring "thon"
3    print(my_str[1:5]) # You get the substring "ytho"
4    print(my_str[0:2]) # You get the substring "Py"
5    print(my_str[4:6]) # You get the substring "on"
```

**Output:**

```
Pyth
thon
ytho
Py
on
```

# Negative Indexing

Negative indexing can be used to access the string from the end.

Consider the example below:

```
1    a = "Hello, World!"
2    print(a[-5:-2])
```

**Output:**

```
orl
```

# Check String:

In order to check if a certain text or character is present in a string, we can use the keywords in or not in.

93

```
1   txt = "A quick brown fox jumps over a lazy dog"
2   x = "uic" in txt
3   print(x)
```

**Output:**

```
True
```

# String concatenation

By concatenating, we mean joining two or more strings to make a combined string. The concept of concatenation is widely used in most of the scenarios as it performs a vital role in logic-building to solve a problem. The strings are concatenated with a plus "+" symbol.

Consider an example in which multiple strings are concatenated to become a single string:

```
1    str_a = "The"
2    str_b = "quick"
3    str_c = "brown"
4    str_d = "fox"
5    str_e = "jumps"
6    str_f = "over"
7    str_g = "the"
8    str_h = "lazy"
9    str_i = "dog"
10
11   complete_string = str_a +" "+ str_b+" "+str_c+" "+str_d+" "+str_e+" "+str_f+" "+str_g+" "+str_h+" "+str_i +"."
12
13   print(complete_string)
```

**Output:**

```
The quick brown fox jumps over the lazy dog.
```

# String functions

Here comes the answer to our question "What we are going to do with these letters?"

Consider the name "jAmEs BonD". Now, we notice that it is not written in title case. Thus, to change the string from "jAmEs BonD" to "James Bond", we have to go through each character of the string and apply string functions to make the entire string look just like we want.

The string functions are used to convert the string in the required format. By using them, we can also make validation rules on strings for our own convenience.

# 1. Boolean methods

In Python, there are some string methods that will result in a Boolean value. They are very useful when playing with a string. They are also helpful when you are creating a form to be filled in by the users. For instance, if you want a user to fill in his/her phone number, we will use a Boolean method that will ensure that the user can only enter numeric values.

Here is a list of some commonly used Boolean methods:

| Method | Use |
|---|---|
|  |  |

| | |
|---|---|
| str.isupper() | Returns true if string's alphabetic characters are all in uppercase. |
| str.islower() | Returns true if string's alphabetic characters are all in lowercase. |
| str.isnumeric() | Returns true if string consist of numeric values only. |
| str.isalpha() | Returns true if string consist of alphabets only. |
| str.istitle() | Returns true if string is in title case. |
| str.ispace() | Returns true if string consists of only whitespace characters. |
| str.isalphanum() | Returns true if string consists of alphanumeric values only. |

*Examples:*

The examples given here will make your understanding clearer. Let's try str.isnumeric().

```
1    number = "6"
2    letter = "python"
3
4    print(number.isnumeric())
5    print(letter.isnumeric())
```

**Output:**

```
True
False
```

Now let's try str.isupper(), str.islower() and str.istitle() methods.

```
1    str_a = "Introduction To Python"
2    str_b = "PYTHON PROGRAMMING"
3    str_c = "hello world"
4
5    print(str_a.istitle())
6    print(str_a.isupper())
7    print(str_a.islower())
8
9    print(str_b.istitle())
10   print(str_b.isupper())
11   print(str_b.islower())
12
13   print(str_c.istitle())
14   print(str_c.isupper())
15   print(str_c.islower())
```

**Output:**

```
True
False
False
False
True
False
False
False
True
```

# 2. The use of len keyword

The '**len**' (short for length) keyword provides the number of characters that a string contains. For example, a string "Python" contains 6 characters ('P', 'y', 't', 'h', 'o', 'n'). Let's consider an example of getting the length of the string "Hello, World!":

```
1    my_str = "Hello, World!"
2    print(len(my_str))
```

**Output:**

```
13
```

# 3. Changing case of a string

The case of strings matters when we have to take care of the data format. In Python, we can capitalize the entire string with just one function, that is **upper()**. In the following example, we convert the string "TwO hEaDs aRe betTeR ThAn OnE" to "TWO HEADS ARE BETTER THAN ONE":

```
1    my_str = "TwO hEaDs aRe betTeR ThAn OnE"
2    my_str_in_caps = my_str.upper()
3    print(my_str_in_caps)
```

**Output:**

```
TWO HEADS ARE BETTER THAN ONE
```

Just like changing an entire string to upper case, we can convert the entire string to lower case as well. In the following example, we are going to convert the same string "TwO hEaDs aRe betTeR ThAn OnE" to "two heads are better than one":

```
1   my_str = "TwO hEaDs aRe betTeR ThAn OnE"
2   my_str_in_small = my_str.lower()
3   print(my_str_in_small)
```

**Output:**

```
two heads are better than one
```

# 4. Replacing a letter or word in a string

If we are curious whether we could replace a letter or a substring in an existing string to form a completely new string, Python gives you the solution. Using the function **replace ()**, we could achieve the solution to the problem. The replace () function takes three arguments:

1) The letter or substring in an existing string;
2) The letter or string that we want to replace;
3) Numbers of times we want to replace the letter or substring (optional).

Let's consider an example in which we have a string "The 2nd world war" and we want to replace the substring "2nd" with the string

"Second". Thus, the string "The 2nd world war" becomes "The Second world war":

```
1    my_str = "The 2nd world war"
2    my_new_string = my_str.replace("2nd","Second")
3    print(my_new_string)
```

**Output:**

```
The Second world war
```

Note that my_str is still the same "The 2nd world war". When we apply the function **replace ()**, it does not change the integrity of the original string, instead, it just makes a copy of that string and performs the replace function to it. Hence, in order to capture the new string, we have to assign it to another variable "my_new_string" so that we could use it for our convenience.

# 5. Splitting a string

By splitting a string, we mean making chunks of strings that are separated by a letter or substring which we have to provide to the function. The **split** () function takes only one argument that is a letter or a substring that works as a splitter of the actual string. Now the question is if the split () function returns many strings as chunks of string, which data type holds the combination of these strings? The **list**. Yes, we get the list of strings separated by a letter or substring when using the **split ()** function. Let's consider a string "The quick brown fox jumps over the lazy dog." which we want to split over a single space " " so that we get the list "['The', 'quick', 'brown', 'fox', 'jumps', 'over', 'the', 'lazy', 'dog.']":

```
1    my_str = "The quick brown fox jumps over the lazy dog."
2    list_of_substring = my_str.split(" ")
3    print(list_of_substring)
```

**Output:**

```
['The', 'quick', 'brown', 'fox', 'jumps', 'over', 'the', 'lazy', 'dog.']
```

# Exercises

**1) Write a program that contains a string:**

> **my_str = "guido van rossum"**

**You have to convert the above string to "Guido van Rossum".**

**Note:  Use upper () or lower () functions and string concatenation only. Finally, display the converted string. Do not use the replace () function.**

**2) Write a program that compares two strings and displays whether they are equal or not. The program should ignore the case of strings.**

**Str_a = "bAskEt"**

**Str_b = "BAskET"**

# Solutions

### Solution of Exercise 1:

```
1   my_str = "guido van rossum"
2   my_str = my_str.split(" ")
3   first_name = my_str[0]
4   first_name_cap = first_name[0].upper() + first_name[1:len(first_name)]
5   last_name = my_str[2]
6   last_name_cap = last_name[0].upper() + last_name[1:len(last_name)]
7   complete_name = first_name_cap +" "+ my_str[1] + " " + last_name_cap
8   print(complete_name)
```

### Solution of Exercise 2:

```
1   str_a = "bAskEt"
2   str_b = "BAskET"
3
4   if str_a.lower() == str_b.lower():
5       print("Strings are same")
6
7   else:
8       print("Strings are not same")
```

# Mini project

**Your task is to convert the string:**

**"jAmEs boNd-iS-OnE-oF-thE-fInEsT-fIcTiOnAL-ChAraCterS-oF-HOlLyWoOD."**

**to:**

**"Commander James Bond is one of the finest fictional characters of Hollywood." using string functions.**

**The program should also tell if the converted string has a length greater than 70.**

Solution:

```
1   my_str = "jAmEs boNd-iS-OnE-oF-thE-fInEsT-fIcTiOnAL-ChAraCterS-oF-HOlLyWoOD."
2   my_str = my_str.lower()
3   my_str = my_str.replace("-", " ")
4   my_str = my_str.replace("james bond", "Commander James Bond")
5   my_str = my_str.replace("hollywood", "Hollywood")
6   print(my_str)
7   if(len(my_str)>70):
8       print("The length is greater than 70")
9
```

# DAY 6

## FILE HANDLING

# What is a file

We need files to store data on our computers. A file is a named location on your disk to store information. The data is stored permanently in non-volatile memory (hard disk).

# File handling

The concept of file handling in python is not as lengthy and complicated as compared to other languages. The important point in python is that it treats a file as a text or a binary. Each line of code is a sequence of characters and collectively they form a text file. There is a special character called End of Line (EOL) that determines the end of a line.

In python, no external libraries are needed to read or write files. There are built-in functions in python for reading, writing and creating files. In this chapter, we will walk through these functions and some other functions to help you understand better.

# Opening a file

Opening a file is very easy in python. We use the built-in function open () to open a file. The open () functions take two arguments i.e. the name of the file e.g. "python.txt" and the other argument is a predetermined mode. These pre-determined modes represent the type of function we want to perform on the file. Though it is not necessary to enter a mode. If you don't enter any mode, then by default python will consider it to be in "r" i.e. reading mode. We will discuss these modes in detail in the next section.

## Basic syntax

Here is a basic syntax to use the open () function.

*open (filename, mode)*

Now consider the following text file, located in the same folder as Python, with the name "python.txt" that has the following text written in it.

```
1    f= open("python.txt", "r")
```

## File Modes in Python

Following are different modes:

**w+** - To create a file if does not exist in library

**w** – To write in a file

**a** – To append a line in the file

**r** – To read a file

**r+** - To both read and write a file

**t** - To open a file in text mode(default mode)

**b** - To open a file in binary mode.

# Naming:

When we load a file, a particular name is given to that file (which is saved in _name_attribute). In case, if it is loaded as top-level characters, the name would be _main_.

In case if it's loaded as a module its name becomes a filename, preceded by the names of sub-packages or packages divided by the dots.

# Creating a file

Now to create a new file, we will again use the open () method with one of the following modes.

"x" – it creates a file and returns an error if the file already exists "a" – it creates a file if the specified file does not exist

"w" --it creates a file if the specified file does not exist

Confused? Don't worry. Let's clear it out with an example.

```
1    f = open("myfile.txt", "x")
```

This command will create an empty .txt file with the name 'myfile'.

# Reading a file
# Reading the complete file

Now in Python, we don't only create a file, but we can also read a file. It is done by calling the file in read mode. It is as easy as opening and creating a file. To read the content of the file we will use read () method.

The code is pretty much self-explanatory so let's go directly to coding.

```
1    f=open("python.txt", "r")
2    if f.mode == 'r':
3        contents =f.read()
4        print(contents)
```

The 'if' condition in this code is used to check that the file open is in read mode. If true, then it will proceed.

# Reading only parts of file

In python, we can also read parts of a file. When read () method reads the whole file, we can also specify the number of characters we want to read in a file. Here is an example if we want to read the first seven characters of "python.txt"

```python
f=open("python.txt", "r")
if f.mode == 'r':
    contents =f.read(7)
    print(contents)
```

# Reading lines of a file

We can also return only one line of the file by using the readline () method.

```python
f=open("python.txt", "r")
print(f.readline())
```

Similarly, if we want to return two lines we can this method twice.

```python
f=open("python.txt", "r")
print(f.readline())
print(f.readline())
```

If we want to read the whole file line by line, we can use a for loop.

```python
f=open("python.txt", "r")
for x in f:
    print(x)
```

Similarly, readlines() method returns a list of lines.

```
1   f=open("python.txt", "r")
2   print(f.readlines())
```

# Writing in a file

Python also allow us to write in a file. We use the same open () function. We add the file name as the first parameter and then for the second parameter, we can use the following two modes:

**w** – To write in a file or to overwrite the existing content

**a** – To append a line at the end of the file

There are various methods just like read function. Let's walk through each method one by one.

## Write to an existing file

In order to write something in an already existing file, we use the append mode i.e. "a". It simply adds a line to the end of the file.

Consider the following example:

```
1   f=open("python.txt", "a")
2   f.write("Appending a line to the file")
3   f.close()
4
5   #to open and read the file after the appending:
6   f = open("python.txt", "r")
7   print(f.read())
```

Now if we want to overwrite the existing file we will use "w" mode. Consider the example.

```
1  f = open("python.txt", "w")
2  f.write("Overwriting the existing file")
3  f.close()
4
5  #open and read the file after the appending:
6  f = open("python.txt", "r")
7  print(f.read())
```

# Write lines to an existing file

We can also write a list of string that will be added as the line to the file. For this purpose, there is a method called writelines (). Consider the following example.

```
1  f = open("python.txt", "w")
2  text_lines = ["Adding line one", "Adding line two", "Adding line three"]
3  f.writelines(text_lines)
4  f.close()
5
6  #open and read the file:
7  f = open("python.txt", "r")
8  print(f.read())
```

# Closing a file

It is very important that you close a file when you are done with it as the changes that you made to a file may not show until you close a file. Probably, by now you have guessed the method that we will use to close the file.

Let's go directly to the example.

```
1   f = open("python.txt", "w")
2   f.write("Overwriting the existing file")
3   f.close()
```

# Splitting lines in a file

We can also split the lines in a file in Python. Splitting is done while considering the whitespaces in a text by default, but we can also set any other character as the criteria for the split. We use the split () method for this purpose.

```
1   f = open("python.txt", "w")
2   content = f.readlines()
3   for line in content:
4       word = line.split()
5       print(word)
```

# Python file methods

There are various other methods to handle a file. Some of them are listed below.

| Method | Use |
|--------|-----|
| detach() | Separates the binary buffer from the TextIOBase and returns it. |

| | |
|---|---|
| fileno() | Used to return the file descriptor (an integer number) of the file. |
| flush() | Used to flush the write buffer of the file stream |
| isatty() | If the file stream is interactive it returns true. |
| readable() | If the file stream is read able it returns true. |
| tell() | It is used to return the current location of the file. |
| writable() | If we can write in the file it returns true. |

# Exercises

1. Create a function to write into a file with a single function call. It should only take a file path and text content as a parameter. Also if the file does not exist it should create new file and overwrite if file already exists. Also, test your function.

2. Create a function to read from a file with a single function call. It should only take the file path and return the contents of it. Also, test your function.

# Solution

1.

```
10    #Function to write to file
11  ▢def WriteFile(path,text):
12  ▢    file = open(path,'a+')
13  │    status = file.write(text)
14  ├    file.close()
15  └    return status
```

2.

```
3     #Function to read file
4   ▢def ReadFile(path):
5   ▢    file = open(path,'r+')
6   │    content = file.read()
7   ├    file.close()
8   └    return content
```

# Mini project

Using the two functions created from exercise creates a program that takes string input from the user and encrypts it and stores the encrypted string into a file. The program should also allow the user to read the file and decrypt it. Search online for encryption algorithms, you have the freedom to choose the algorithm of your choice

# DAY 7

## DATA STRUCTURES & OBJECT-ORIENTED PROGRAMMING

This is the last day and since we have covered all the basic concepts of python and I hope that you have grasped them pretty well by now, let's take an overview of some advanced concepts. It will help you in taking insights of object-oriented concepts in programming.

# Data Structures:

Data Structures are also known as collections and are one of the very basic concepts in programming and computer science as it is helpful in writing efficient programs in all languages. They are used to store data and to organize it efficiently.

They are used to hold the data together and store related data together. For example, when there is more than one variable but they all have similar meanings (like the age of kids, scores of students, etc.) then we use various types of collection which is supposed to acts as a single variable containing all the data.

Python has four built-in data structures:

- ❖ List
- ❖ Set
- ❖ Tuple
- ❖ Dictionary

# List

A list is a collection that has ordered and changeable members. It allows the duplication of its members. Python uses square brackets to denote a list. Consider the example below:

```
1    list = ["a", "b", "c"]
2    print(list)
```

*Output:*

```
['a', 'b', 'c']
```

We can also access each item on the list individually. See the example below:

```
1    list = ["a", "b", "c"]
2    print(list[2])
```

*Output:*

```
c
```

To change the value of any item in the list we can use the index number of that item as shown in the example below:

```
1    list = ["a", "b", "c"]
2    list[2] = "d"
3    print(list)
```

*Output:*

```
['a', 'b', 'd']
```

To loop through all the items in the list we can use for method. See the example below:

```
1    list = ["a", "b", "c"]
2    for x in list:
3        print(x)
```

*Output:*

```
a
b
c
```

To check if any item exists in a list, we can use the 'if" condition.

```
1    list = ["a", "b", "c"]
2    if "a" in list:
3        print("a is present in the list")
```

*Output:*

```
a is present in the list
```

We can also check the length of the list i.e. the number of items present in the list. There is a built-in function called len() in Python for this purpose.

```
1    list = ["a", "b", "c"]
2    print(len(list))
```

*Output:*

```
3
```

To add an item to the list, we can use the built-in function append().
This will add the new item at the end of the list. See the example
below:

```
1    list = ["a", "b", "c"]
2    list.append("d")
3    print(list)
```

*Output:*

```
['a', 'b', 'c', 'd']
```

In case, we want to add an item at any certain index of the list we
can use the built-in function insert(). See the example below:

```
1    list = ["a", "b", "c"]
2    list.insert(1, "d")
3    print(list)
```

*Output:*

```
['a', 'd', 'b', 'c']
```

To remove any item from the list there are several methods that
are mentioned below.

remove ()

pop ()

del

clear ()

Let's see all the four methods to remove an item from the list.

**Remove ():**

```
1    list = ["a", "b", "c","d","e","f"]
2    list.remove("d")
3    print(list)
```

*Output:*

```
['a', 'b', 'c', 'e', 'f']
```

**Pop ():**

```
1    list = ["a", "b", "c","d","e","f"]
2    list.pop()
3    print(list)
```

*Output:*

```
['a', 'b', 'c', 'd', 'e']
```

**del:**

```
1    list = ["a", "b", "c","d","e","f"]
2    del list
```

*Output:*

The list will be deleted completely.

**Clear ():**

```
1    list = ["a", "b", "c","d","e","f"]
2    list.clear()
3    print(list)
```

*Output:*

[]

**There are several other methods in Python that we can use on the
list. Some of them are mentioned below:**

| Method | What do they do |
|--------|-----------------|
| append() | It appends an element at the end of the list |
| clear() | It clears all the elements from the list |
| copy() | It returns a copy of the list |
| count() | It returns the number of elements with the specified value |
| extend() | It appends the elements of a list (or any iterable), to the end of the current list. |
| index() | It returns the index of the first element with the specified value |
| insert() | It adds an element at the specified position |
| pop() | It removes the element at the specified position |
| remove() | It removes the item with the specified value |
| reverse() | It reverses the order of the list |
| sort() | It sorts the list |

# Tuple

A tuple is a collection of data that is unordered and unchangeable.
Parentheses are used to represent tuples in Python. To clear the
concept let's try an example.

```
1  tuple = ("a", "b", "c")
2  print(tuple)
```

*Output*

```
('a', 'b', 'c')
```

121

We can also access individual items of the tuples and do most of the tasks similar to that of a list. Here are a few examples:

```
1   #declaring a tuple
2   tuple = ("a", "b", "c", "d", "e", "f", "g", "h", "i")
3
4   #accessing an item in the tuple
5   print(tuple[1])
6
7   #negative indexing
8   print(tuple[-1])
9
10  #specifing the range of items in the tuple
11  print(tuple[2:5])
12
13  #specifying range of negative index
14  print(tuple[-4:-1])
15
16  #looping through a tuple
17  for x in tuple:
18      print(x)
19
20  #checking for an item in the tuple
21  if "b" in tuple:
22      print("Yes, 'b' is in the tuple")
23
24  #length of the tuple
25  print(len(tuple))
26
27  #deleting the tuple
28  del tuple
29  print(tuple)
```

*Output*

```
b
i
('c', 'd', 'e')
('f', 'g', 'h')
a
b
c
d
e
f
g
h
i
Yes, 'b' is in the tuple
9
<class 'tuple'>
```

However, there are certain actions that are either difficult or impossible to perform on a tuple as it is immutable (unchangeable) type.

Some of the examples of such actions are:

1.  Changing Tuple values

2.  Adding an item to a tuple

3.  Deleting an item from the tuple

However, to change an item in a tuple we can first convert it into a list which is a mutable type, and then change the list and convert it back to a tuple. See the below example for help:

```
1   x = ("a", "b", "c")
2   y = list(x)
3   y[1] = "d"
4   x = tuple(y)
5
6   print(x)
```

*Output*

```
('a', 'd', 'c')
```

# Creating a tuple with only one item

In Python, we cannot create a tuple with a single item unless we add a comma at the end or else Python won't recognize it as a tuple.

See the example below:

```
1   tuple = ("a",)
2   print(type(tuple))
3
4   tuple = ("a")
5   print(type(tuple))
```

*Output*

```
<class 'tuple'>
<class 'str'>
```

# Set

A set is a collection of unordered and un-indexed items. The set in Python is denoted with curly braces.

Here is an example of a simple set:

```
1    set = {"a", "b", "c"}
2    print(set)
```

*Output*

```
{'b', 'a', 'c'}
```

Now, in the output, notice that the order in which the items appear is not the same as we denoted in the actual set. This happens because the set is a collection of unordered items.

Let's first go through the common actions that we can perform on a set.

```
1   #declaring a set
2   set = {"a", "b", "c", "d", "e", "f", "g", "h", "i"}
3
4   #adding one item to a set
5   set.add("j")
6   print(set)
7
8   #adding more than one item to a set
9   set.update("k","l")
10  print(set)
11
12  #looping through a set
13  for x in set:
14      print(x)
15
16  #checking for an item in the set
17  if "b" in set:
18      print("Yes, 'b' is in the set")
19
20  #length of the set
21  print(len(set))
22
23  #removing an item from a set
24  set.remove("j")
25  print(set)
26
27  #deleting the set completely
28  del set
29  print(set)
30
31  #joining two sets
32  set1 = {"a", "b" , "c"}
33  set2 = {1, 2, 3}
34
35  set3 = set1.union(set2)
36  print(set3)
37
38  #or
39  set1.update(set2)
40  print(set1)
```

Output

```
{'a', 'i', 'f', 'c', 'd', 'h', 'g', 'j', 'b', 'e'}
{'a', 'i', 'l', 'f', 'c', 'k', 'd', 'h', 'g', 'j', 'b', 'e'}
a
i
l
f
c
k
d
h
g
j
b
e
Yes, 'b' is in the set
12
{'a', 'i', 'l', 'f', 'c', 'k', 'd', 'h', 'g', 'b', 'e'}
<class 'set'>
{'a', 'b', 1, 2, 3, 'c'}
{'a', 'b', 1, 2, 3, 'c'}
```

Now we cannot access an item in a set by referring to its index as the items in the set do not have any index. We can't change the items in the set, but we can add the new items.

# Dictionary

A dictionary is a collection of unordered but changeable and indexed items. They are denoted just like sets but they have a key-value pair.

See the example below:

```
1  dict = {
2      "brand": "HP",
3      "model": "Pavilion",
4      "year": 2018
5  }
6  print(dict)
```

*Output*

```
{'brand': 'HP', 'model': 'Pavilion', 'year': 2018]
```

Let's first go through the common actions that we can perform on a set.

```
1   #declaring a dict
2   dict =  {
3       "brand": "HP",
4       "model": "Pavilion",
5       "year": 2018
6   }
7
8   #accessing an item in the dict
9   x = dict["model"]
10  print(x)
11
12  #or
13  x = dict.get("model")
14  print(x)
15
16  #changing values of item in a dict
17  dict["year"] = 2019
18  print(dict)
19
20  #adding one item to a dict
21  dict["color"] = "silver"
22  print(dict)
23
24  #looping through all keys in a dict
25  for x in dict:
26      print(x)
27
28  #looping through all values in a dict
29  for x in dict:
30      print(dict[x])
31
32  #or
33  for x in dict.values():
34      print(x)
35
36  #looping through all keys and values in a dict
37  for x, y in dict.items():
38      print(x, y)
```

```
40    #checking for an item in the dict
41    if "model" in dict:
42        print("Yes, 'model' is one of the keys in the dict dictionary")
43
44    #length of the dict
45    print(len(dict))
46
47    #removing an item from a dict
48    dict.pop("model")
49    print(dict)
50
51    #deleting the dict completely
52    del dict
53    print(dict)
54
55    #joining two dicts
56    dict1 = {"a", "b" , "c"}
57    dict2 = {1, 2, 3}
58
59    dict3 = dict1.union(dict2)
60    print(dict3)
61
62    #or
63    dict1.update(dict2)
64    print(dict1)
```

## Output

```
Pavilion
Pavilion
{'brand': 'HP', 'model': 'Pavilion', 'year': 2019}
{'brand': 'HP', 'model': 'Pavilion', 'year': 2019, 'color': 'silver'}
brand
model
year
color
HP
Pavilion
2019
silver
HP
Pavilion
2019
silver
brand HP
model Pavilion
year 2019
color silver
Yes, 'model' is one of the keys in the dict dictionary
4
{'brand': 'HP', 'year': 2019, 'color': 'silver'}
<class 'dict'>
{'b', 'c', 1, 2, 3, 'a'}
{'b', 'c', 1, 2, 3, 'a'}
```

# Nested dictionaries

A dictionary can also contain a dictionary in it as an item.

```
1  parent = {
2      "child1" : {
3          "name" : "Jane",
4          "year" : 1998
5      },
6      "child2" : {
7          "name" : "John",
8          "year" : 2001
9      },
10     "child3" : {
11         "name" : "Tom",
12         "year" : 2005
13     }
14 }
```

# Object-Oriented Programming in Python:

First, the question arises that what is object-oriented programming? Object-oriented programming (OOP) is a language model in which we further organize our programs in form of objects rather than functions or logic. An object here can be defined as a data field with unique attributes and behaviors.

A very good example of an object is a human being. Humans have attributes like name, address, phone numbers, etc.

Following are the programming languages that are object-oriented:

❖ Python

- ❖ Java

- ❖ JavaScript

- ❖ C++

- ❖ Ruby

- ❖ PHP

- ❖ Scala

- ❖ Visual Basic .NET

# Object:

Let's clear the concept of an object. As I told you earlier that, an object here can be defined as a data field with unique attributes and behaviors. So, we know that the basic characteristics of an object are: **attributes** and **behavior**.

Consider an object car. What will be the attributes of the car? Car's model, Seating capacity, Car's color, number of doors, number of wheels, etc.

Similarly, list down the behavior of the car like it can start, stop, accelerate, show how much fuel is missing, etc.

The behavior of an object is also called the method.

# Class:

This takes us to the next step that is a class. Consider a class as a blueprint from which individual objects can be created. Take the previous example of a car. We defined an object car but in the real world, we find many objects like car. All the cars have the same basic attributes and are built from the same set of blueprints with similar components.

So, a class is basically a blueprint for objects.

Let's look at the example below:

```
class Car:

    # create class attributes
    name = "c500"
    make = "mercedez"
    model = 2017

    # create class methods
    def start(self):
        print ("Car Engine is started")

    def stop(self):
        print ("Car Engine is switched off")
```

In the above example, we created a class named car and then added the attributes name, make and model. Then we created two methods start() and stop().

Now, we can also create objects from the above class. For example:

```
16    # Creates car_a object of Car class
17    car_a = Car()
18
19    # Creates car_b object of car class
20    car_b = Car()
```

# Attributes:

We have already seen an example in which we defined some attributes of an object. Now, remember that attributes can be broadly classified into two types i.e. Class attributes and instance attributes.

The difference between both is that the class attributes are shared by all objects whereas instance objects are only for the instance.

In the above examples, we defined the class attributes. Now let's see an example of instance attributes.

```
1    class Car:
2
3        # instance attributes
4        def __init__(self, name, make, model):
5        self.name = "c500"
6        self.make = "mercedez"
7        self.model = 2017
```

# Methods:

Methods are the behaviors of the objects. They are used to implement the functionalities of the object. We created the methods start () and stop () in the above example. We can call the methods by their objects and we can also call them directly.

*Calling a method by the object*

In order to call a method, we need to create the object first. Let's continue with the above car example where we created an object car_a. Now we can use them to access the methods of the class.

```
class Car:

    # create class attributes
    name = "c500"
    make = "mercedez"
    model = 2017

    # create class methods
    def start(self):
        print ("Car Engine is started")

    def stop(self):
        print ("Car Engine is switched off")

# Creates car_a object of Car class
car_a = Car()

#Calling the methods by objects
print(car_a.name)
print(car_a.make)
print(car_a.model)
```

**Output:**

```
c500
mercedez
2017
```

*Calling a method directly*

To call a method of a class directly, we use static methods. To declare the static method, we use @staticmethod to specify it. It is called a descriptor. Now let's see that example again.

```python
class Car:

    # create class attributes
    name = "c500"
    make = "mercedez"
    model = 2017

    # create static methods
    @staticmethod
    def car_details():
        print("This is a car class")

# Calling the static methods
print(Car.car_details())
```

**Output:**

```
This is a car class.
```

# Constructors:

Constructors are special methods in a class. They are called by default whenever we create an object of a class. A keyword __init__ is used to create a constructor. It will become clearer once you look at the following example:

```
1   class Car:
2
3        # create class attributes
4        car_count = 0
5
6        # create constructor method
7        def __init__(self):
8            Car.car_count +=1
9            print(Car.car_count)
10
11   car_a = Car()
12   car_b = Car()
13   car_c = Car()
```

**Output:**

```
1
2
3
```

Here in this example, we created a class car with one attribute i.e. car_count. The constructor class increments this count whenever the class is called and prints the value.

# Access Modifiers:

In python, access modifiers are used to modify the default scope of a variable. These access modifiers are:

❖ Public

❖ Private

❖ Protected

# Public access modifier

Variables with public access modifiers can be accessed anywhere.

# Private access modifier

Variables with private access modifiers can be accessed only inside the class.

# Protected access modifier

Variables with protected access modifiers can be accessed within the same package.

Let's consider the same example.

```
1  class Car:
2      def __init__(self):
3          print ("Engine started")
4          # declaring a public variable
5          self.name = "corolla"
6          # declaring a private variable
7          self.__make = "toyota"
8          # declaring a protected variable
9          self._model = 1999
10
11  car_a = Car()
12  print(car_a.name)
13  print(car_a.make)
14  print(car_a.make)
```

**Output:**

137

```
Engine started
corolla

AttributeError: 'Car' object has no attribute 'make'
```

From the output, we can clearly see that only the public variable is printed.

Now we have almost covered the basic concepts of OOP in Python. Let's discuss the three pillars of OOP also known as PIE: Polymorphism, Inheritance, and Encapsulation.

# Inheritance

Inheritance in python is just like the inheritance in the real-world where a child inherits some traits from its parents along with some traits of his own. It is more of an IS-A relationship. As car **is a** vehicle.

In Python, the concept of inheritance is like a class (child/derived class) can inherit some traits from another class (parent/base class).

Let's look at an example:

```
1    # Create Class Vehicle
2    class Vehicle:
3        def vehicle_method(self):
4            print("This is parent Vehicle class method")
5
6    # Create Class Car that inherits Vehicle
7    class Car(Vehicle):
8        def car_method(self):
9            print("This is child Car class method")
10
11   # Create Class Cycle that inherits Vehicle
12   class Cycle(Vehicle):
13       def cycleMethod(self):
14           print("This is child Cycle class method")
15
16   car_a = Car()
17   car_a.vehicle_method() # Calling parent class method
18   car_b = Cycle()
19   car_b.vehicle_method() # Calling parent class method
```

**Output:**

```
This is parent Vehicle class method
This is parent Vehicle class method
```

Here we created a parent class Vehicle and two child classes Car and Cycle. A parent class can have multiple children and a child class can have multiple parents. This is called multiple inheritances. To see an example of multiple parents, see the example given below:

```
1   class Audio:
2       def audio_method(self):
3           print("This is parent audio class method")
4
5   class Video:
6       def video_method(self):
7           print("This is parent video class method")
8
9   class CellPhone(Audio, Video):
10      def cell_phone_method(self):
11          print("This is child CellPhone class method")
12
13  cell_phone_a = CellPhone()
14  cell_phone_a.audio_method()
15  cell_phone_a.video_method()
```

**Output:**

```
This is parent audio class method
This is parent video class method
```

Here the child class cell_phone has access to both parent classes'

method i.e. video_method() and audio_method().

# Polymorphism

Polymorphism means having multiple forms. Polymorphism relates

to an object's capacity to act in various respects in the framework

of object-oriented programming. Polymorphism is introduced in

programming by overloading methods and overriding methods.

# Method Overloading

Method overloading relates to a method's estate to act in distinct respects based on the number of kinds of parameters. Look at a straightforward instance of an overloading technique.

```
1   # Creates class Car
2   class Car:
3       def start(self, a, b=None):
4           if b is not None:
5               print (a + b)
6           else:
7               print (a)
8
9   car_a = Car()
10  car_a.start(10)
11  car_a.start(10,20)
```

**Output:**

```
10
30
```

In the above example, if we pass a single argument to start () method it will simply print it. If we pass two parameters to it, it will then add them and print the result.

# Method Overriding:

The overriding technique is a way to include a method in the child class with the same name as in the parent class. The method definition varies in the classes of parent and child, but the name remains the same. Consider the example below:

```python
# Create Class Vehicle
class Vehicle:
    def print_details(self):
        print("This is parent Vehicle class method")

# Create Class Car that inherits Vehicle
class Car(Vehicle):
    def print_details(self):
        print("This is child Car class method")

# Create Class Cycle that inherits Vehicle
class Cycle(Vehicle):
    def print_details(self):
        print("This is child Cycle class method")

car_a = Vehicle()
car_a. print_details()

car_b = Car()
car_b.print_details()

car_c = Cycle()
car_c.print_details()
```

**Output:**

```
This is parent Vehicle class method
This is child Car class method
This is child Cycle class method
```

# Encapsulation

The simple way of defining the encapsulation is the concept of data hiding in programming. It means that a class should not have access to another class's data. This access should be provided via some methods. It gives us more control over coupling.

In Python, this controlled access to data is provided by access modifiers. As we have already discussed the concept of access modifiers so now, we will see its properties in action. We will declare the variables private here in the example below:

```python
class Car:

    __maxspeed = 0
    __name = ""

    def __init__(self):
        self.__maxspeed = 200
        self.__name = "Corolla"

    def drive(self):
        print('Maxspeed is: ' + str(self.__maxspeed))

car_a = Car()
car_a.drive()
car_a.__maxspeed = 10  # will not change variable because its private
car_a.drive()
```

**Output:**

```
Maxspeed is: 200
Maxspeed is: 200
```

We see that the maxspeed did not change. Now, if we want to access these private attributes, we have to create set methods for them.

```
1   class Car:
2
3       __maxspeed = 0
4       __name = ""
5
6       def __init__(self):
7           self.__maxspeed = 200
8           self.__name = "Corolla"
9
10      def drive(self):
11          print('Max speed is: ' + str(self.__maxspeed))
12
13      def setMaxSpeed(self, speed):
14          self.__maxspeed = speed
15
16  car_a = Car()
17  car_a.drive()
18  car_a.setMaxSpeed(320)
19  car_a.drive()
```

**Output:**

```
Max speed is: 200
Max speed is: 320
```

# Exercise:

1)  Define a class, which has a class parameter and have the same instance parameter.

2)  Define a class named Shape and its subclass Square. The Square class has an 'init' function which takes a length as an argument. Both classes have an area function that can print the area of the shape where the Shape's area is 0 by default.

3) Define a class named Rectangle which can be constructed by a length and width. The Rectangle class has a method that can compute the area.

# Solution:

## The Solution to exercise 1:

```
1   class Person:
2           # Define the class parameter "name"
3           name = "Person"
4
5       def __init__(self, name = None):
6               # self.name is the instance parameter
7               self.name = name
8
9   jeffrey = Person("John")
10  print "%s name is %s" % (Person.name, john.name)
11
12  nico = Person()
13  nico.name = "Nico"
14  print "%s name is %s" % (Person.name, nico.name)
```

## The Solution to exercise 2:

```
1   class Shape(object):
2       def __init__(self):
3           pass
4
5       def area(self):
6           return 0
7
8   class Square(Shape):
9       def __init__(self, l):
10          Shape.__init__(self)
11          self.length = l
12
13      def area(self):
14          return self.length*self.length
15
16  aSquare= Square(3)
17  print aSquare.area()
```

The Solution to exercise 3:

```
1   class Rectangle(object):
2       def __init__(self, l, w):
3           self.length = l
4           self.width  = w
5
6       def area(self):
7           return self.length*self.width
8
9   Rectangle_a = Rectangle(5,6)
10  print Rectangle_a.area()
```

# Mini Project:

Your task is to create a deck of cards class. The deck of cards class should use another class internally, a card class. Your requirements are:

- ❖ The Deck class should have a deal method to deal with a single card from the deck

- ❖ After a card is dealt, it is removed from the deck.

- ❖ There should be a shuffle method that makes sure the deck of cards has all 52 cards and then rearranges them randomly.

- ❖ The Card class should have a suit (Hearts, Diamonds, Clubs, Spades) and a value (A,2,3,4,5,6,7,8,9,10, J, Q, K)

Solution:

```python
from random import shuffle

class Card:
    def __init__(self, suit, value):
        self.suit = suit
        self.value = value

    def __repr__(self):
        return "{} of {}".format(self.value, self.suit)

class Deck:
    def __init__(self):
        suits = ['Hearts','Diamonds','Clubs','Spades']
        values = ['A','2','3','4','5','6','7','8','9','10','J','Q','K']
        self.cards = [Card(suit, value) for suit in suits for value in values]

    def __repr__(self):
        return "Cards remaining in deck: {}".format(len(self.cards))

    def shuffle(self):
        if len(self.cards) < 52:
            raise ValueError("Only full decks can be shuffled")
        shuffle(self.cards)
        return self

    def deal(self):
        if len(self.cards) == 0:
            raise ValueError("All cards have been dealt")
        return self.cards.pop()
```

```
from random import shuffle

class Card:
    def __init__(self, suit, value):
        self.suit = suit
        self.value = value

    def __repr__(self):
        return "{} of {}".format(self.value, self.suit)

class Deck:
    def __init__(self):
        suits = ['Hearts','Diamonds','Clubs','Spades']
        values = ['A','2','3','4','5','6','7','8','9','10','J','Q','K']
        self.cards = [Card(suit, value) for suit in suits for value in values]

    def __repr__(self):
        return "Cards remaining in deck: {}".format(len(self.cards))

    def shuffle(self):
        if len(self.cards) < 52:
            raise ValueError("Only full decks can be shuffled")
        shuffle(self.cards)
        return self

    def deal(self):
        if len(self.cards) == 0:
            raise ValueError("All cards have been dealt")
        return self.cards.pop()
```

# GETTING INTO THE REAL WORLD

## Python Tips and Tricks:

Here are some essential Python programming tricks.

## Swapping two numbers

```
1   x, y = 10, 20
2   print(x, y)
3   x, y = y, x
4   print(x, y)
```

## Reversing a String

```
1   a ="Python Programming"
2   print("Reverse is", a[::-1])
```

## Creating a single string

```
1   a = ["Python", "is", "Fun"]
2   print(" ".join(a))
```

# Chaining of Comparison Operators

```
1   n = 10
2   result = 1 < n < 20
3   print(result)
4   result = 1 > n <= 9
5   print(result)
```

# Print the path of the imported module

```
1   import os;
2   import socket;
3
4   print(os)
5   print(socket)
```

# Return Multiple Values from Functions

```
1   def x():
2       return 1, 2, 3, 4
3   a, b, c, d = x()
4
5   print(a, b, c, d)
```

# Find the Most Frequent Value in a List

```
1   test = [1, 2, 3, 4, 2, 2, 3, 1, 4, 4, 4]
2   print(max(set(test), key = test.count))
```

# Printing a string n times

```
1   n = 5;
2   a ="Python";
3   print(a * n);
```

# Transposing a matrix

```
1   mat = [[1, 2, 3], [4, 5, 6]]
2   zip(*mat)
3   [(1, 4), (2, 5), (3, 6)]
```

# Combining two lists

```
1   list_1 = ['a', 'b', 'c', 'd']
2   list_2 = ['p', 'q', 'r', 's']
3
4   for x, y in zip(list_1,list_2):
5       print x, y
```

# Common Python Questions and Answers:

**Q: What is the difference between a compiler and an interpreter?**

A: See Day 1.

**Q: What is the difference between a list and a tuple?**

A: See Day 2.

**Q: What are the local and global variables in Python?**

**A:** See Day 4.

**Q: Is Python case sensitive?**

A: Yes, it is a case sensitive language.

**Q:  What is the difference between Python arrays and lists?**

A: See Day 2.

**Q:  What are the functions in Python?**

A: See Day 4.

**Q: What is __init__?**

A: See Day 7.

**Q: What is self in Python?**

A: Self is an instance of an object in a class. See Day 7.

**Q: How does break works in python?**

A: See Day 3.

**Q: How do you write comments in Python?**

A: See Day 2.

**Q: How will you convert a string to lower case?**

A: See Day 5.

**Q: What are some operators in Python?**

A: See Day 2.

**Q: What is a dictionary in Python?**

A: See Day 2.

**Q: What does len() function do?**

A: See Day 5.

**Q: What are some built-in types of Python.**

A: See Day 2.

**Q: Does Python have the OOPs concept?**

A: See Day 7.

**Q: Explain inheritance with an example.**

A: See Day 7.

**Q: How do we create a class in Python?**

A: See Day 7.

**Q: Does Python support multiple inheritances?**

A: See Day 7.

**Q: How does python make use of access modifiers?**

A: See Day 7.

# Python Project Ideas:

## Dice Rolling Simulator

This project includes, as the name indicates, composing a program that simulates rolling dice. When the program starts, a range between 1 and 6 will be selected randomly. (Or whatever other integers you prefer— it's up to you to have the number of sides on the die.) The program will print the number. It will then ask the user if they would like to roll again. You will need to set a min and max range that the dice can produce. You will also need to look into random function.

**Note:** Take a look at Day 2 and Day 3 of the book.

## Guess the number

It is just like the above project. It will also use the random module in Python. The program will generate a number randomly within a given range and it will ask the user to guess the number. The user should be able to input the number. If the entered number is wrong, then the program should be able to tell if it is too high or too low from the number that they have to guess. If the user guesses correctly a positive indication such as YOU WIN should appear on the screen.

**Note:** Take a look at Day 2 and Day 3 of the book.

# URL Shortener

The primary goal is to shorten URLs and then redirect users to the initial URL when visiting the shortened URL. The users will enter the initial URL in the software, resulting in the fresh, reduced URL. To do this, you can generate the characters for the shortened URL using a combination of random and string modules.

You will need to save the original and shortened URLs in a database as users visit the shortened URL days, months, or even years later. The application controls whether the URL remains and redirects to the initial when a request goes in, or it redirects to a 404 section.

**Note:** Take a look at Day 2 and Day 5 of the book.

# Create a quiz application

The Quiz Application will provide people with questions and will expect the correct responses to those problems. Think of the application of the Quiz as a type of questionnaire. The primary goal of this initiative is to put quizzes and get users to solve them. As a result, users should be able to ask questions, and other users should be able to reply to those questions.

Users will simply upload a text file with questions and answers. It should have a specified format that you can decide so that the application can convert it into a quiz.

**Note:** Take a look at Day 6 of the book.

# Create a calculator

The calculator is a great project for beginners. The goal is to make a simple calculator that asks the user for input and then prints the output accordingly. It is up to you to add more functionalities such as GUI (Graphical User Interface).

**Note:** Take a look at Day 2, 3 and Day 5 of the book.

# Bibliography:

Guru99. (2018). *Python Tutorial for Beginners: Learn Python Programming in 7 Days*. Retrieved from Guru99: https://www.guru99.com/python-tutorials.html

programiz. (2019). *Learn Python Programming*. Retrieved from Programiz: https://www.programiz.com/python-programming

Python Software Foundation. (2019). *Python 3.7.4 documentation*. Retrieved from Python Software Foundation: https://docs.python.org/3/

w3schools. (n.d.). *Python Tutorial*. Retrieved 2019, from w3schools.com:
https://www.w3schools.com/python/default.asp

Made in the USA
Middletown, DE
22 December 2019